Enjoy!

A CELEBRATION OF
JENNIFER PATERSON

Edited by
Christopher Sinclair-Stevenson

ISIS
LARGE PRINT
Oxford

First published in Great Britain 2000
by Headline Book Publishing

Published in Large Print 2001 by ISIS Publishing Ltd,
7 Centremead, Osney Mead, Oxford OX2 0ES, by arrangement
with Headline Book Publishing, a division of Hodder Headline

British Library Cataloguing in Publication Data
Enjoy!: a celebration of Jennifer Paterson. – Large print ed.
1. Paterson, Jennifer – Appreciation 2. Cooks – Great Britain
– Biography 3. Women cooks – Great Britain – Biography
4. Large type books
I. Sinclair-Stevenson, Christopher
641.5'092

ISBN 0-7531-9682-4 (hb)
ISBN 0-7531-9683-2 (pb)

Printed and bound by Antony Rowe, Chippenham and Reading

ACKNOWLEDGEMENTS

I am extremely grateful to all the contributors; to Charles and James Paterson, Clare Asquith, the Revd Charles Sinnickson, Robert Geary and the *Oldie*, the *Daily Telegraph*, the *Spectator* and Corbis Images for providing illustrations; and to Celia Kent for being a patient and sympathetic editor.

CONTENTS

INTRODUCTION

The compilation of *Enjoy!* should have been as easy as falling off a baron of beef. Instead it provided more pitfalls than a detective story.

What, for a start, is it? Certainly not a tribute, not nearly serious enough. Emphatically not a Festschrift. Jennifer would have hooted with derision. So, a celebration it is.

Then, what about the contributors? I wanted to gather a mixture of friends, perhaps family, colleagues. So there is a hefty section of *Spectator* writers: editors, literary editors and people who really made the wheels turn (no names, no pack drill). Jonathan Routh and Anthony Blond represent Jennifer's raffish early days before journalism and then television snapped her up. Richard Ingrams gives us Lord Gnome's imprimatur, something Cardinal Hume would undoubtedly have supplied (through the Brompton Oratory). And, of course, Clarissa Dickson Wright and Patricia Llewellyn could hardly have been absent.

In many ways, however, it is Jennifer's friends — Tom Hartman and Katharine MacDonogh and Glynn Boyd Harte — who offer some of the most intimate sketches of her. Through their eyes we see a human being, a very human being.

I thought it would be nice if Jennifer herself could be present in these pages, so I selected a few receipts from her last idiosyncratic cookery book, *Seasonal Receipts*. A couple of these are actually linked to contributors. Some give glimpses of Jennifer's revered saints. Some are merely outrageous. Funny, quirky, the sharp fingernails almost out of the gauntlets. Just like her . . .

A celebration indeed. Enjoy!

Christopher Sinclair-Stevenson

These Foolish Things

Ned Sherrin

Jennifer's encyclopaedic knowledge of old standard songs and her willingness to sing them right through with gusto suggested to me that she might enjoy being remembered by a limping parody of one of her favourites (with apologies to Eric Maschwitz):

> A ruby gash of lipstick lights the vision,
> A hoot of laughter or of gay derision,
> These bold and chunky rings,
> These foolish things remind me of you.
> The chugging sidecar and the swerving scooter,
> The jewelled helmet o'er the noble hooter,
> The tried and true receipts,
> These scrumptious treats remind me of you.
> Each anniversary the phone
> Would ring and you would sing
> That corny "Happy Birthday" thing.
> The "perfect poached egg" with the tidy edges,
> The fulminations at the boring "veggies",
> The splendid things you could do
> To oxtail stew remind me of you.

The herbs and sauces that make taste buds flutter,
Excess of cream and then excess of butter,
And ah, how glad I am
A paschal lamb reminds me of you.
The feasts of saints and the appropr'ate dishes,
The magic you could work on loaves and fishes,
And kissing card'nal's rings,
These Cath'lic things remind me of you.

Up there I guess St Peter now
Is sampling your pilau;
And if he moans he can expect a row.
The finest products from God's finest dairy,
A few "Our Fathers" and a lone "Hail Mary",
Oh, how the ghost of you sings!
These foolish things remind us of you.

Early Memories

James Paterson
C. J. Paterson
Verily Anderson
Ronald Creighton-Jobe
Jonathan Meades
Jonathan, Jodi and
Christian Routh

Jennifer's brothers James and Charles introduce us to the very young and the often turbulently growing up Jennifer (and we also see her through her nanny's eyes — she deserves our sympathy). One can already see some of the characteristics which were to be elaborated in later life: a certain wilfulness, stubbornness, and teenage eccentricity.

But also the first faint glimmerings of faith, here addressed by Father Creighton-Jobe from Jennifer's beloved London Oratory. The two Jonathans, Meades and Routh, open the door to more public goings-on. Jonathan Meades, the discriminating food writer and

3

novelist, lifts the veil on What Jennifer Did At the Girls' School where she performed the duties of Matron in a somewhat unusual manner. Jonathan Routh remembers Jennifer's vital contribution to his famous, some would say infamous, series *Candid Camera*.

On the Beach

James Paterson

My sister Jennifer was four years older than me. Four years can be a very divisive gap, especially when you go off to boarding school at the age of seven. Add to this the turbulence that beset our family, like so many, during the war years — both of us spent some time at our respective schools because, for a time, we had no family home — and you have two siblings who grew up barely knowing one another. Even when we did happen to be at home together the age difference meant that we had virtually no shared interests, occupations or friends. Moreover, by the time I was ten Jennifer had already taken leave of her convent school and, ever a precocious girl, moved off into — for me — the strange and sophisticated world of Art School, working for the Windsor Rep as an ASM, looking after Canadian servicemen in the Knights of Columbus canteen in Lower Regent Street, and heading off, when she was seventeen, to join my father in Hanover and Berlin, with the Army of the Rhine. All this while I struggled with my Euclid and French subjunctives under the watchful eyes, and strong right arms, of Benedictine monks in darkest Huntingdonshire.

There remain, however, some snap-shot recollections of those times: a very freckle-faced Jennifer on the beach at Winchelsea and Camber; Jennifer and our many female cousins getting dressed for their first "long dress" dance at some grand hotel in Hastings — and practising the "Lambeth Walk". I don't actually remember Jennifer feeding me, aged two, a garden snail, in shell, in our garden in Rye — but she always said, somewhat defensively I feel, that I seemed to enjoy it. Rather gloomy holidays in Nairn in the early part of the war, when our father was at Fort George, and Jennifer, then keen to become a tutu'd circus rider, drawing endless horses and ballet dancers. Charades on the lawn of the Old Manor House (our home for a few wartime years) on the banks of the River Mole near Hampton Court — with Jennifer, in the role of a condemned witch, being flung, screaming, into the river by an astonishingly caparisoned mob, led by a mitred bishop (Uncle Anthony I suspect), just as a very sedate punt-load of elderly trippers rounded the bend in the river.

Or Jennifer dressing and making me up as a girl (rather entrancingly I recall — I was possibly just twelve) to introduce me to our father, who had just returned on leave from some unlikely spot like Strathpeffer. He was a large, kilted, Seaforth Highlander with a fine red moustache, but musical and otherworldly. Of course, he was completely deceived and made some gallant overtures to the "pretty young visitor" before Jennifer's barely stifled whoops of glee gave the game away.

In 1947 and '48 Jennifer lived with our parents in the British sector of Berlin. My father, an ardent musicologist, balletomane and aspirant composer, had some unlikely job that involved, *inter alia*, the staging of concerts, operas and ballets for the sometimes only marginally enthusiastic British soldiery in Berlin. I used to come out, with trainloads of other schoolchildren, for the holidays, and for a while, and from a slightly more mature viewpoint, was able to witness Jennifer's activities at close hand. She was about nineteen, vivacious, sportive (a great swimmer and enthusiastic tennis player and skier) and attractive. She had a great number of followers, both British and American, not least because she used to act for the US forces Little Theatre and had some good parts.

The 11th Hussars (or "Cherrypickers") were part of the British Garrison in Berlin, and Jennifer seemed to spend a lot of time with their elegant, magenta-trousered young subalterns. She was part of a "Gang of Three" — the other two being Hardy, the daughter of an American Admiral, and Sim, the daughter of a Canadian General. There were not a lot of unattached young women among the Allied contingents in Berlin at that time (and the "non-fraternisation" rule was still in force with regard to the German population), so these three were very much in demand and, I would say, had a very good time indeed. As far as I am aware this was the only time in her life when Jennifer came close to getting married. She had an admirer whom we as a family all knew and liked. I think he was serious about Jennifer; she may have been serious too, but she was also insouciant and probably considered that she was much too young to "settle down". She once told me that when young men got serious and started proposing marriage, possibly on bended knee, she would get a "fit of the giggles". Deflating, to say the least, for the genuflecting gallant.

Jennifer did a very nice thing for me in Berlin. She knew a lot of Americans through her theatrical work. One couple invited her to their house in the US sector, to stay the night and go dancing at the Harnackhaus, which I believe was a rather grand sort of officers' club. Jennifer took me, aged fifteen, along too. On reflection, that was action beyond the call of duty for a senior sister; not only that, but she procured for me, if that is quite the right word, an American "bobby-soxer" date to take to the dance. They played Glenn Miller's music — and her name was Jane. Thank you, Jennifer.

Which brings us to Italy, Taormina to be exact, which is the other place where I spent some time with Jennifer. After Berlin, when my father left the Army in 1948, he and my mother moved to Italy — the better to commune with his balletic muse (and there was also the very minor consideration that his oddly sourced dollar income went further, and was taxed less, in lire). Jennifer really departed the parental home after Berlin, and went off on a series of mother's help-type jobs; initially, I think, to Portugal, with one of the famous English port families.

But in the summer of 1952 Jennifer must have been at a loose end and she went to Taormina, to where our parents had moved, my father having found the Ligurian coast too noisy. I went there also, on leave from Sandhurst. Jennifer became a "beach girl" — Mazzaro beach was devoid of hotels in those days — and rapidly fell in with the American dietician, Gayelord Hauser, and his entourage, who had a house at the end of the beach. He and his partner Brownie, a distinguished-looking, silver-headed man, became devoted to Jennifer, and she to them. This was perhaps the first of her friendships of this nature — an intriguing strand in her life that was to persevere.

At the same time she had a boisterous following of good-looking and distinctly macho young Sicilians called Franco, Bruno and the like, with whom she danced, swam and played beach ball. It was a good time for her — and for me, as I trailed along in her wake. Rather as she had done in Berlin, she took me to a party. One of the well-known dynastic American families had rented a villa nearby; it was fancy dress and I went as a pirate, wearing on my head a black stockinet cap belonging to Jennifer. During the revels there may conceivably have been some sort of encounter with one of the young female dynasts in a less well-lit part of the garden — memory is extremely vague at this distant remove. Anyway the pirate's hat was lost, forgotten and never recovered. I do recall, however, with startling clarity, my sister's displeasure the following morning.

After Taormina we really lost touch. Jennifer went, I think, though my chronology for her gets hazy here, off to be a mother's help with our Aunt Fara, who had married a baronet, who at that time was commanding an army unit in Benghazi. They had several children and Jennifer stayed with them for a year or so. Later, she worked as a sort of secretary and factotum for Fiore Henriques, the renowned sculptress. I was once beside Jennifer and Fiore at a funeral in Westminster Cathedral. Fiore wore a black Homburg hat, Jennifer wore some black millinery exoticism; both sang in rich baritone voices, at a considerably lower pitch than myself. I know that Jennifer travelled to Nassau with Fiore and revelled in the pink coral beaches. She always liked a beach, and pink was her favourite colour.

Not long after this must have come her stint as "matron" at Padworth College — a girls' finishing school in Berkshire. We sent one of our daughters there three years later — it turned out to be not one of our better scholastic moves. As a former diplomat I shall skip lightly over Jennifer's sojourn as a housekeeper at the Ugandan High Commission's bachelor quarters. As with several other of her employments, she left suddenly — but not, I gather, on this occasion as a result of *her* wantonness. I know she worked for several years with a nice family in Montpelier Square, and was happy there. I think it was after that she started going around London on her small Honda motorcycle, cooking dinner for people. Then came her *Spectator* job and the radio and TV roles.

People have often said to me how lovely it must have been to have a sister who cooked all those scrumptious dishes. Sadly, I have to reply that life and circumstances decreed that I never partook of one of Jennifer's mouth-watering feasts such as she and Clarissa prepared for "little jockeys" and Scottish lumberjacks. I cannot remember her ever doing any cooking in the early years. My mother, as Jennifer so often liked to point out, did not cook, at least in any serious way, and meals in our house in the war years were scratch affairs — a good deal of spam and powdered egg — usually cooked by one of the many people either billeted on us or just passing through or, great treat, when our grandmother's cook, Rose, came over to do a real meal on Sundays. Jennifer's culinary skills must have been gathered after she left home. An agglomeration of dishes was learnt in Portugal (her passion for "anchovies with everything"?), Benghazi (where Aunt Fara says Jennifer picked up a lot from the Libyan "cookboy"), and at her various establishments thereafter. All this, together with a demand for "real" ingredients of high quality and absolutely no truck with anything so ludicrous as calorie-counting and, one might say, good taste and a natural flair.

My problem in writing about Jennifer after we parted in Taormina is that I spent the next forty years in the Army and the diplomatic service, more often abroad than at home, and even when at home not actually living in London. So we met infrequently. I do recall writing to Jennifer from the New Territories in Hong Kong, in about 1954, when I was trying, as "Food Member", to think of appealing menus for an increasingly abusive officers' mess. She sent me a very good "receipt" for lemon meringue pie — which rather baffled our Chinese cook but, I think, after one or two embarrassing trials, turned out quite well. She also used to send me the words of some of her vast repertoire of songs — Noël Coward and the like — to use at regimental concerts, pantomimes and such. As time went on, however, our lives grew increasingly disparate, and as she got more and more involved in the bohemian, and latterly media, worlds in which she thrived, the sort of rather conventional "service" existence that my brother Charles and I lived — with our wives and largish families — must have appeared humdrum indeed. She was not really a "family-orientated" person — though she was very good at remembering everyone's birthday and ringing up to sing a birthday greeting. While she hardly was a doting aunt to her ten nephews and nieces, she would, from time to time, "field" one or more of my children on their way from school to whatever distant capital we were residing in and, to their delight, take them to unsuitable films at London cinemas.

When I returned to England, on retirement, in late 1992, I was hoping to see more of Jennifer, and that Christmas she and Charles and I did have a very successful — and noisy — reunion at our house in Walmer. Thereafter, however, Jennifer's "late" career started to take off, and soon gathered meteoric speed, leaving little time for family gatherings; not Jennifer's wildest delight at the best of times. We were, of course, delighted for her, and heard with amazement (from our relations and correspondents) how popular she and Clarissa had become — in places as diverse as Fremantle, Fort Lauderdale and Pietermaritzburg. Jennifer was evidently enjoying it immensely. It was a sad and cruel blow therefore that laid her low while she was still at the top of her form. Still, she was ever one to "grasp the moment" and grasp it she did — *con brio*. She would have been very bored to have had to give up her cigarettes, her vodka, her flamboyant life — and to suffer the indignities of old age. As I'm sure she would have planned it (but she seldom planned anything), she got off the bus while it was still running — and running well, God bless her.

Jennifer Mary Paterson

C. J. Paterson

A word about our father. His father was an "old China hand", returned to England late in life, married a London beauty (the "best lady violinist in town") and became an elderly parent. They were well off, so our father, Robert Paterson, was brought up to be a dilettante without much encouragement to work for a career. He wound up at Sandhurst in 1914 and was soon at the Front with the Seaforth Highlanders. The family is Scottish. He came out of the war with a good MC (almost a VC) but wounded and with nerves fairly shattered. After various false starts, his father got him a position in China with the Asiatic Petroleum Company, which he joined in Nanking in 1921 or so. Meanwhile this lonely and nervy man had met our mother, Josephine Bartlett, one of twelve children in a rumbustious and rather arty family. They were married in St Joseph's Church, Kowloon, in 1924, I think. It was not done in those days to get married in firms like the APC until one was thirty, so there was a bit of trouble.

I was born in Tsingtao in 1926 and ten months later we all came home for leave and Jennifer's birth on 3 April 1928. We then went back to Tientsin in northern China, where we lived until 1932. Jennifer and I had an amah, of course, whom I remember taking us to the local park and swimming pool and with whom we spoke Chinese. Sometimes we were rowed, *en famille*, along the local river in a punt, a splendid craft for family picnics, and I have a distinct memory of Jennifer, in a yellow dress, falling off the bow one day and being rescued towards the stern by the punt coolie. Funnily enough her appearance, like that of a drowned rat, has remained with me when so much else has gone.

Mother said we lived at 4 Hong-Kong Road. It seemed a reasonable house and the grown-up expatriates amused themselves with energy and imagination. A lot of expeditions to ancient temples, amateur theatricals, clever parties and so on. When I got to see the house, or at any rate 4 Hong-Kong Road, a few years ago, it was nothing like anything I remembered. Still, I'm now five foot three and in those days I might have made three foot six, so perspectives would differ.

Other memories are centred on a summer bungalow we had at Shanhai-kwan, where the Great Wall goes into the sea. There were several bungalows in our area and Jen and I would go to play with their children. I recall there being boats and a splendid quarry-type railway along which the bigger boys would propel us in small trucks. I think there was another amah there, the one we called "Crazy Amah" as she was supposed to scratch herself all over with broken glass each morning and she ate jellyfish. We used to collect them for her along the beach in our small wheelbarrows. There was a junk harbour along the beach from us and we would occasionally get aboard a junk and be fed suspect food, much to the consternation of the grown-ups.

There were also leave camps for the legation garrisons in Peking and we were especially pleased with the Italians, who gave the best parties. My mother probably had quite a romance going with one of the officers, Luigi, who was very kind to us and who eventually became my younger brother's godfather.

Our final journey south from the Great Wall to Tientsin was marked in my mind by our passing endless cattle trucks full of Chinese troops going up into Manchuria to fight the Japanese.

Leave must have again been due as we soon boarded a tender to go out over the bar to meet the *Doerflinger*, of the Norddeutscherlloyd Line, which was to take us home. She was not at the rendezvous and we spent a night in a serious storm aboard the tender amid ghastly scenes of seasickness. My father took us up to the boat deck, where we stood in the wind, so we weren't as badly affected as some. In the morning we went aboard a passenger vessel for restoration. For some reason J and I were put in the Captain's cabin, where she, probably we, distinguished ourselves by eating all the Captain's fruit.

Those two-month trips were enormous fun for the grown-ups, with splendid dinners and dances every night. But we were firmly put to bed by the amah, who curiously enough came back to England with us, and were occasionally the cause of dramas when we escaped and hid in good places to watch the fun. Punishments were severe. We saw the Botanical Gardens in Singapore and the netted-off swimming areas in Aden, and in Port Said we were entranced by the little boys who dived for coins from their boats. Eventually we got to the Hook of Holland and caught the ferry to Harwich. That was the first bit of England we really took in. The kippers on the train to London were superb.

After a while we settled in Rye in rather a nice house overlooking the Gun Gardens and the River Rother, and right away our younger brother, James, was born. Apparently J and I spoke Chinese fluently and were often in trouble for using terrible swear words to the local shopkeepers if they didn't follow the Chinese custom of giving children little presents. I'm told we pinched a lot of things that we thought were set out as presents from which to choose. Humiliating visits by our mother returning stuff to shops with profuse apologies about her awful children ensued.

Our father had not come home with us, having to finish something, and when he did come home he had been made redundant, so that was the end of China and indeed employment for him until he rejoined his old regiment, the Seaforths, on the approach of another war in 1938. Heaven knows what we lived on but we moved into very modest accommodation, the amah went home and, surprisingly, we had for several years an Irish nurse who married into a local family who had been smugglers for many generations.

Jennifer and I went to the Providence Convent in the High Street (now Woolworths) and became very tied in with local children, including the daughter of the proprietor of the famous Mermaid Inn in Watchbell Street. I remember J taking part in such tests of skill as the three-legged race and the slow bicycle race. I also remember the hill, which seemed so endless, up which we toiled home; unbelievable to see it now, a shortish, fairly gentle slope. Our treat was being taken to Winchelsea beach by one of my mother's brothers, who would turn up in one of the cars that could be had for £5 in those days. Sliding roofs that we could stand looking through — great fun.

Rye and Winchelsea were full of agreeably mad people. We even had the novelist Radclyffe Hall (*The Well of Loneliness*) living a few doors away. At Winchelsea a man "controlled the tides" with a fine array of zigzag railway lines that went out to sea. Eventually we rented a house called The Ark on the beach for the summer and we were often joined by other parts of our vast family for the holidays. Once Jennifer ran across my line of sight when I was shooting an arrow at a target. Got her in the left temple — lots of blood! Mother was beside herself with rage, not so much because of the wound, which was slight, but because the blood ruined a new coat that J was wearing.

I went off to St Augustine's Abbey School, Ramsgate, in 1935 and I suppose a couple of years later Jennifer came to the Convent of the Assumption at nearby Pegwell Bay. We boys who had sisters at the Convent would process over to see them on a Sunday, a popular move as the girls got off Vespers. Much rushing about the convent gardens making fun of each other. The Rev. Mother, Madame Rita, had been at school with our mother at the Assumption in Kensington Square, but even so the time came when she had to expel Jennifer for "disrupting the even tenor of the school". In the family we always heard that she was running some kind of "protection racket" and was found standing near to a girl with a tooth out and looking suspicious with a roller skate in her hand. No doubt quite apocryphal. Later she would say that the "boys" got all the available money for their education and not her. She omitted to mention being expelled.

So, where are we? In 1937 we moved to Hastings and into a larger house. Grandfather Paterson, whom we didn't know (he had cut Father off with a shilling for marrying a Catholic), had died and his wife, Lilian, became our parents' responsibility. The estate allowed a small income to help cover the cost. Lilian's beauty having faded, she had taken to the bottle and many were the embarrassments fielded by our parents. J and I would take an interest in her treasures and found her fascinating, but she is supposed to have thrown all Mother's jewellery down the lavatory.

Come the war we moved first to a houseboat on the Thames near Taggs Island in which we enjoyed the 1940 blitz, and then into a ropy old house in East Molesey rejoicing in the name of The Old Manor House, one of my mother's magical fixes through local friends. She even fixed us up with several boats. Father was not around at this time, being used as a trooping major in ships taking soldiers to the Far East. Mother's attitude to bombing was "Oh, I long for death!" So we never took shelter of any kind. There were a couple of near misses. A stick of bombs just missed the houseboat and fortunately the one that went in by the bow was a dud.

At The Old Manor House, later in the war, we sat in the garden and watched the "doodlebugs" flying over. Some cut out apparently right overhead but they landed several hundred yards away. My memory is of cheerful holidays. Our house was a home from home for a great many relations and friends on weekend passes from their units; I think we had twenty-eight relations in uniform. By 1940 I was at naval college and so sported a uniform too and was guilty of some big "line shoots" in the community.

Not quite sure when Jennifer was expelled from the Assumption; about 1942, I suppose. Anyway she then went to a very agreeable school round the corner run by two pretty young women. Very lucky, my brother and I thought, as we suffered the ghastliness of wartime food at our cold boarding schools. But local distractions soon meant little progress at school and so J went off to Kingston Art School. That didn't last long either.

I was posted to the Pacific in 1944 and that was really the last time that I was in any way closely involved with J's life. When I came home in 1946 my father had some splendid job in Berlin resuscitating the ballet and opera — a much-loved figure in his kilt and with a canny ability to get food from the NAAFI to starving German artistes. No heating in the theatres, so everyone went around with overcoats and blankets. Of course, J was one of the very few there and so had a lovely time; I joined up with them for two weeks' leave on the Baltic at Travemünde. But reality had eventually to be faced. My father's army time was running out, so he paid J back £100 that she had lent him (from a legacy) and dispatched her as though he was providing a munificent dowry for a splendid wedding, rather hoping she would be gone for good.

This started Jennifer on her long career of helping families with their children and household tasks, beginning with our Aunt Fara, who was accompanying her husband to Tripoli, where he was to command his regiment. From that time on I hardly saw her again unless we happened to meet on holiday somewhere.

Odd memories. Jennifer worked for Norman Kark of *Courier* magazine (*inter alia*) as an office girl of some sort. That must have been soon after the war. She was on very good terms with the woman in her office and got me to do my Frankenstein impression for her. I had been at school with Norman's son, Austen (who eventually became the head of BBC Overseas Programmes at Bush House), but even so, when Jennifer insisted on going to some appointment of her own rather than sticking to her work, she was sacked. Rather her trouble: her wishes came first.

I met her with her eccentric employer, Fiore Henriques, an Italian sculptress. J enjoyed Fiore's sensational rows with restaurateurs who tried to stop her using their establishments while wearing trousers. She never wore anything else. She had some female companion. We didn't really know about lesbians in those days but if we had we would not have recognized it; not that Jennifer was involved.

I never met the Ugandans J worked for but I did see her two or three times with the nice millers whose firm made Spiller's Shapes dog biscuits, among other things. She looked after a nice little house opposite Harrods in Montpelier Square and seemed very much at home with the family and its friends. Another family was the Peploes. Willie Peploe had an art gallery in Bond Street and his wife, Clo-Clo, was a considerable artist, and a great friend of a couple of my uncles. The children, as I remember them, were spoilt.

My father died in Venice in 1964 and my mother came home and moved in with my uncle, Anthony Bartlett, opposite the front door of Westminster Cathedral in Ashley Place. That block was pulled down to make way for the plaza, so they moved round the corner to Ashley Gardens. Anthony was very involved with the cathedral, serving Mass every day and being the Cardinal's "gentiluomo", a sort of flag-lieutenant, a rôle he'd inherited from his father in 1936. He was now on his sixth cardinal. Anthony was and is a saint. After some years of my mother, who at least arranged amusing little parties, Jennifer came to the end of one of her jobs — looking after Violet Cripps, a one-time Duchess of Westminster, who, like others, got the sack when no heir appeared. She had just died. In fact we had known the family for many years. I was saying: J was given refuge in Anthony's flat in the spare bedroom and there she stayed for almost twenty years until her own death.

My mother moved out when she became a bit too old and incompetent and came to be looked after by me and my wife. Jennifer stayed on, eventually got the job of doing the directors' lunches at the *Spectator*, and that led on to her connections with people like Richard Ingrams, articles in magazines about cooking and restaurants, and so to Patricia Llewellyn and the *Two Fat Ladies* programmes.

Although J had rather cut herself off from our brother James and me, as she was not geared to family luncheons and children, we exchanged greetings cards and phone calls on high days and holy days and, every now and then, James and I would call on her to do our duty. We always got on all right but she would never come out to lunch with us as our idea of a reasonable pub was a bit low-grade for her after all her free meals in grand restaurants while writing critiques. What really upset us was that despite all her cooking, fame and increased wealth she seldom if ever made the slightest effort for her uncle and host, who would come in from some late welfare work and have to get himself some supper. They existed in a state of armed neutrality and she left him nothing in her will despite his having paid almost all the bills for her during her occupation of his spare bedroom. Still, he bore no hard feelings and when she died he took part in arranging her splendid funeral.

The Nanny's Tale

Verily Anderson

Jennifer Paterson was one of my charges when, as a student during the holidays, bar-minding was not on for a parson's daughter. Anyway, I liked children, so I suppose nowadays one would say I baby-sat Jennifer and, it seemed, her countless little brothers and sisters.

In those days only Norland nurses or family heirlooms were called nannies. Au pairs had not yet been invented. Mothers' helps were considered middle-class acquisitions, when middle class meant living on a ribbon development, not as now, in a stately home with a string of racehorses.

Jennifer would have been the last to admit being associated with a mother's help, and certainly her home was a far cry from London's Great West Road. It was a disintegrating, genuinely Tudor three-up-and-one-more-down-than-ever house within tottering, toddling and crawling distance of Rye's historic church, though the Patersons themselves were devout Roman Catholics. I became very fond of the mother, who was well ahead of her time in believing pram-straps to be unnecessary, and even prams. Not much traffic toiled up the cobbled streets but there was a river. "All babies can swim, if they try," I learnt. Miss Mapp, alias Mr E. F. Benson, was then Mayor of Rye.

Memorable was my first evening, when the parents said they were going out for a drink. There was no mention of putting anyone to bed, so I presumed it would be half an hour down at the Mermaid, which was then a sixpence-a-pint local. Jennifer immediately offered to show me how she could lead all ages of her family up one side of a bookcase, along the top and down the other side, not once but often. Jennifer's chubby face became rosier and her plaits more rampant as she warmed to the task of going up the opposite way to the others, passing them over *The Dialogues of Plato* in four volumes and coming down over *Decline and Fall*.

She then showed me how to have a "stir-up". Although the cupboards were bare of anything much more than the pea and a bean that her mother told me they lived on while her husband composed concertos, the kitchen was soon in chaos and the smaller children were slowly sliding asleep off their chairs. The minutes ticked by and then the hours, but Jennifer was the last to slump. I picked them up in order of size and wove my way up to fill the beds above. Jennifer was only eight and sturdy, though not as heavy as in due course, but the stairs wound perilously. The parents returned soon after 1a.m. They'd had a marvellous time with the Duchess of Bedford.

Years later I was walking along Kensington High Street when a taxi pulled up, the door opened and a chirpy young voice from within called out, "Verily, no less! It's your own little Jenny from Rye! Hop in! We're going to lunch at Claridges!" There was no way I could have recognised Jennifer, but she had seen my occasional appearances on black-and-white television — teaching Brownies to cook, curiously.

"How I wish I could! I'm on my way to the library and I've left all my starving children alone in the park."

"Don't worry! They'll love it and anyway Christopher Isherwood's paying" — by which time she was eating lumps of sugar out of her handbag. "It's my doctor's idea to take away my appetite. Six before every meal." I wished I could have gone, if only to see whether the lumps of sugar worked. She told me the next day, "A complete waste of calories and it didn't do the lobster Thermidor any good either. But the old taste-buds had picked up by the stuffed goose, and the chestnut meringues were delectable."

After that I saw her mother more often than I saw Jennifer, who was just back from Benghazi and was looking for a new job.

"I suppose . . ." I began. "No, she wouldn't want to — er — be a me, like I was to your family?"

"My dear," said her mother noticing what I wore. "Even if you could afford the wages she demands, nobody I know could afford the ingredients."

Jennifer Paterson the Catholic

Ronald Creighton-Jobe

I first sensed that all was not well with Jennifer one Sunday morning about two months before her death. She had looked tired and unwell for some time, but her arrival on her moped before the High Mass, with a stentorian shout of welcome to everyone in the courtyard, had become almost a part of the dominical ritual. On that particular Sunday there was an ominous silence. At the beginning of Mass, during the singing of the Asperges, when the congregation is sprinkled with holy water, there was no basso profundo participation from her usual place in the row of seats in front of the pulpit, affectionately known as "hags' passage". Was she filming in some exotic place? Was she terrorizing a community of nuns or a gaggle of Boy Scouts? At any rate she was not there, and she was missed. I rang her at home immediately after Mass and found a rather confused and frankly rather frightened Jennifer on the other end of the line. I ordered her to the doctor and, surprisingly, she complied. Within weeks I was hearing her last confession and administering the Sacrament of the Sick, or, as she preferred to call it, "the last rites, darlin'."

I had first met Jennifer thirty years earlier when I entered the London Oratory as a novice. As such, I was discouraged from speaking to parishioners. Judging this to be sheer nonsense, Jennifer ignored the proscription and enfolded me in one of her formidable bear hugs whenever our paths met. Fortunately no broken bones were ever incurred, perhaps one of many minor miracles to be recounted if ever her cause for sainthood is introduced. St Jennifer the Cook? Stranger things have happened in the history of the Catholic Church.

Theologians divide the Church into the Church Triumphant in heaven, the Church Suffering in purgatory, and the Church Militant here on earth. Jennifer belonged, most decidedly, to the last category. Woe betide the suggestion that some trendy hymn should sully the dignity of divine worship. Heaven forfend if some priest or nun of advanced views should inveigh against indulgences or pilgrimages. They would have the wrath of Miss Paterson to contend with, and that was no mean deterrent. Strong men have grown pale when faced with her highest of dudgeons. She loved the rhythms of the Church's year and the externals of her public liturgy, but this was only a part of the essential place her Catholic faith held in the fabric of her life. Her faith might have been simple in one sense, but it was not uncomplicated, because Jennifer Paterson was certainly not an uncomplicated person, in spite of the façade which she had erected to protect her from prying bystanders. Even her friends could enter only so far into her inner life. A priest is more fortunate and privileged in this respect but must always exercise the most determined discretion in speaking of another's soul.

It is clear that her life had not been without suffering. She was by no means a dullard, but her academic skills were limited or perhaps never properly developed. Her experience of education by nuns was a disaster for both sides involved. She was never a beauty, but she had an idiosyncratic charm and verve, which flowered later in her famous television appearances. But in some ways she remained immensely vulnerable, and this she hid away, not always very successfully. If anyone came too near, the danger signals could be glimpsed by the discerning and the portcullis was firmly lowered to repulse the intruder. It was, of course, typical of her generation or rather the generation before her, for Jennifer, for all her exuberance, was actually intensely conservative. She did not appreciate innovation, most particularly in her life as a Catholic.

In this she echoed her uncle, Monsignor Francis Bartlett, who for many years was administrator of Westminster Cathedral, to which her family had always been connected in various ways. Monsignor Bartlett, who possessed a mordant wit, had struggled to maintain the dignity of the daily conventual Mass and choir offices after the cataclysmic changes following the Second Vatican Council and was a fount of knowledge on things liturgical and historical. He was removed shortly after the appointment of the late Cardinal Hume, and the gradual changes in the life of worship at the cathedral were not greatly to his liking, and certainly not to the tastes of his redoubtable niece, who, of all the family, was closest to him. His leaving the cathedral was the signal for Jennifer's migration to the London Oratory, which remained her spiritual home for the rest of her life. Her uncle's death was a blow to her. She always spoke of him with deep affection and resembled him in her stoic acceptance of disappointment and later in her brave acquiescence to her last illness. Neither suffered fools gladly. Francis Bartlett was once heard to describe a candidate for the episcopacy as "not just a yes man, but a yes *please* man . . ." Jennifer relished the phrase.

With her cathedral background Jennifer arrived at the London Oratory with some suspicion. Who were these extraordinary collection of clerics and how would they take to her? More to the point, how would she take to them? In fact, it was love at first sight.

Jennifer had a strong sense of history even if her mastery of dates was rather less developed. She was attracted to the founder of the London Oratory, St Philip Neri, whose life spanned most of the sixteenth century. By birth a Florentine, he was to become the second apostle of Rome, winning souls through his attractiveness of character and never losing that independence of mind and eccentricity which are so typical of his native city. He abhorred pomposity and was a lover of practical jokes, but underlying it all was a profound seriousness and a thirst for souls. He used art and music to glorify God, and was the patron of Palestrina and Animuccia. In other words, he was a saint very much after Jennifer's heart — "your dotty founder", as she was fond of saying, with obvious affection.

But she did not only adopt the oratory church as her spiritual home. She also took the community under her wing. She was never intrusive, considering religious houses of men rather in the same light as gentlemen's clubs. They were for men, not women. Feminism was another of her anathemas. When she could help practically, she did so. For three Christmases she cooked Christmas lunch for the Fathers. The first year established the pattern. She would arrive on her moped promptly at 8.45 in the morning, with the first course, her delicious salmon mousse, deposited in the box at the back of her little two-wheeler. When taxed with the possibility that there might not be enough time to cook two large turkeys, the response was characteristic: "I'm the cook, darlin', leave that to me." When asked what she needed, she replied with a bon mot, now famous: "A bottle of vodka and a good-looking young man." The first could be provided, the second was rather more difficult to oblige with.

Sounds of increasing merriment could be heard from the large but primitive kitchen, reaching a basso profundo climax as the alcohol took its effect. Lunch was ready on the dot of 1.15, the turkey and all its trimmings done to perfection and the Fathers assembled. Into this claustral decorum chaos exploded. Ladies are not allowed into the community refectory, but the door would be thrown open, a raven-haired head appear round the corner and a stentorian cry of "Happy Christmas, darlings" would herald Jennifer's departure for her own

Christmas lunch. After that, Christmas at the oratory would never be the same. Although at that stage of her life she was poor as a church mouse, she never asked for a penny. It was done purely out of love.

But St Philip Neri was not the only favourite saint of Jennifer. Her articles and "receipts" in the *Spectator* often made mention of the saints in the calendar of the week, ranging from holy virgin martyrs to venerable monastic virtuosos. One of her favourites was St Simon Stylites, who spent many years in solitude on the top of a pillar. This feat of asceticism raised many practical questions for Jennifer, some of which were not printable, but amusing nonetheless. True to her intensely Catholic vision of life, these were not just figures from the past. She believed firmly in the communion of saints and their intercessory role in the lives of the faithful. She invoked them for their particular specialities: St Anthony of Padua for lost articles, St Jude for hopeless cases and St Christopher for her beloved moped. One felt that with Jennifer they sometimes had to work overtime. She never seems to have been breathalysed and that is a miracle in itself. When *Two Fat Ladies* was about to be launched she brought the large and rather terrifying motorbike and sidecar to the oratory to be blessed. It had to be done properly, the priest in his *cotta*, stole and biretta, with, as she said, "lashings of holy water", as if it were part of one of her receipts. There were some near misses and mishaps during the filming sessions afterwards, but no real disasters — "and He shall give His angels to watch over your ways".

There is no doubt that Jennifer Paterson could do and say the most appalling things. She often said exactly what came into her mind at the moment. It is also true that this could be wounding and some friendships did flounder on the rocks of this lack of discretion. Some maintain that this was due to a degree of malice. It may be true, but on the other hand she could be capable of great compassion and thoughtfulness. Many was the time that the telephone rang with a request from Jennifer to visit someone seriously ill in hospital or in need of advice or spiritual succour. As always, it was expressed in her inimitable forthright manner and spiced with less than tactful comments about the person concerned, but it proceeded from a genuine sense of Christian charity. In spite of her formidable talents as a conversationalist — indeed there was sometimes an incessant flow — she could be an attentive listener and a shrewd purveyor of good sound advice. She claimed that illness bored her. In fact, as with most of us, it frightened her and when she was called upon to face her own fatal illness it was remarkable how, after her first fearful reaction, she accepted the challenge of her own death with remarkable fortitude.

Jennifer knew that she was far from well for some months before she was diagnosed with terminal cancer. At first she attributed her exhaustion to the gruelling pace of her filming and the travel involved in it. By the time she was admitted to the Chelsea and Westminster Hospital the disease had spread everywhere and there was little to be done. She sent for her confessor, was given the Sacrament of the Sick, and promptly improved dramatically. It was not so much that she was physically better, but that grace had intervened to strengthen and sustain her for the six weeks left to her to live. The sacramental life of the Church was at the very heart of her life with God and her fidelity to it throughout her life was now to bear astonishing fruit. She was at peace with God and was preparing to meet Him.

She received visitors royally in her room in the hospital, dispensing largesse from her large stock of gifts, champagne for others (she preferred something stronger), caviare, soup from the Prince of Wales. Seldom was a sick room more lively and hilariously chaotic. But all the time there was an underlying seriousness of purpose. She was dying and she was determined to do it well. She was praying for the grace of what the old manuals of spirituality call "a good death".

When it did come, it happened suddenly. She had a fall in her room which precipitated a crisis. The faithful friend who came every morning with her newspaper and cappuccino found her in a pitiable state. She was dying and she knew it, and she prayed to all her beloved angels and saints to help her. It was a real rendering of a soul to its creator. She died as a Christian might, conscious to the end, with the holy name on her lips.

Her funeral at the oratory was extraordinary. The great neo-baroque church was full to overflowing. Some of her requests had to be modified. Her motorcycle helmet was there but not on the coffin. She had wanted Verdi's *Requiem*, but that was impossible since the music had never been performed liturgically, but it was all she would have wanted and loved. The music of Mozart's *Requiem* alternating with austere plainsong filled the church. The sacred ministers were vested in black and gold. The Church's ancient language carried the prayers of the Mass heavenwards to God, imploring His mercy: "*Requiem æternam dona eis, Domine*", "Eternal Rest grant unto her, O Lord." Such a strange thought — Jennifer at rest — but the Christian's life is always a yearning for union with God and we are never at rest until we abide in Him, sharing His triune life in heaven.

Jennifer was intensely practical. She knew she needed prayers, and the Mass in Catholic doctrine is the most perfect prayer of all, that offered by the eternal Son of God on our behalf. As her coffin was carried out, the choir intoned the chant of farewell: "May the angels lead you to paradise." One felt that paradise would be receiving a considerable challenge with Jennifer's arrival.

Photographers had been kept firmly out of the Mass, but a phalanx of them were awaiting the appearance of the cortège as it emerged from the church. To their obvious pleasure one of the famous helmets appeared, carried by a suitably lugubrious undertaker. Jennifer would have relished the moment. Can the holy souls in purgatory see their own funerals? In this case, probably not, as it would have given her too much pleasure. In the Catholic tradition there is no such thing as a memorial service. In the Mass we pray for the repose of a soul. We had done so with all the sombre glory at the Church's disposal for a brave woman who loved her faith. In the end perhaps there is no more fitting epitaph.

Someone remarked that the Requiem seemed more like a canonization than a funeral. This was the sort of nonsensical comment that Jennifer would have hated. She was not a saint and she knew it, but she was a good woman full of great courage, with a God-given capacity for love.

When her will was read, it was discovered that she had remembered many of her friends with generous benefactions as well as the Oratory Choir. Jennifer had no sense of money, although she was pleased to have some at the end of a life marked by what is euphemistically called "genteel poverty". She wondered from time to time what would happen to her in old age. God was kind to her. He took her two months after the initial diagnosis, but with time to prepare, and without her suffering any significant pain. She would have appreciated, indeed savoured, the fact that she died on the feast of St Lawrence, deacon and martyr, who was slowly roasted to death on a gridiron and who for his pains was declared patron saint of cooks. What a meeting that must have been when the two encountered each other in heaven. "May the angels lead you into paradise." God grant that prayer to you, dear Jennifer.

Matron was Jennifer

Jonathan Meades

My 1950s were full of Jennifers. I mean that although Jennifer Paterson was formidably individualistic, evidently inimitable, a one-off, *sui generis* and all that, she was those things at a personal level. Socio-economically she was a type, almost the last of a type: she was getting on for a generation younger than her precursors, who were my mother's age: b. 1910-15. I grew up surrounded by these Jennifers. My mother collected them and might, I suppose, have been like them had she not had a husband.

They were spinsters, war widows, divorcees — a rare breed in those days. One had even borne an "illegit" (an ugly epithet but the contemporary usage). They were powerful characters, middle- or upper middle-class by birth, intelligent, outspoken, defiantly untwee, mostly deficient in formal education, mostly unqualified for anything other than the housewifery which had lately eluded them. Despite the presence offstage of well-heeled and often fairly grand relations they were perennially on their uppers. Occasionally there was talk of a man friend but these men friends were invisible men. One, a radio producer, had more than one man friend and led a fast life. I knew this because her home, atypically, was a flat and flats still retained the etiquette attached to them sixty or seventy years previously. More usually they tended neither to own property nor to have a sufficiently reliable income to rent. They moved around a lot, taking live-in jobs or ones that at least provided accommodation.

Matron at a public school for boys who couldn't get into the public school of their parents' choice, perhaps: a position which my father jocularly and ungallantly ascribed to Doreen P—'s having been the headmaster's "groundsheet" when he was a naval officer. Companion to an author of a certain age: for four Christmases on the trot my parents received an effusively signed copy of Compton Mackenzie's latest, but then Lucy H— left his employ to move back south and that particular strain of unreadability ceased.

Now and again one might demonstrate her entrepreneurial ineptitude by helping to open a language school or lending a hand at running a pub and ending up even more out of pocket than when she had embarked on the misadventure. As Muriel Spark had it, "all the nice people were poor". And they sometimes had to do a flit. Gentlefolk? Maybe. But distressed — never! For all their pecuniary worries and their concerns that the covert sources of school fees might dry up they were a spirited bunch who signally disallowed themselves outward signs of despair. Putting a brave face on it was in the grain. The next cloud would be the one. And in the meantime there's always gin and It, Seniors, the races.

The correspondence between Jennifer and these occasionally calamitous women may be frailer than I suppose. (I am not after all certain that the standard c.v. presented in the papers as a profile with its standard accompaniment of a Greek beach photo was anything more than the usual accretion of former cuttings.) But I initially met her long before telly celebrity was thrust upon her in the last three years of her life, long before the papers had to recycle each other's half-truths to explain the season's cathode phenomenon. And from the first she struck me as being like the younger sister of one of Mummy's *galère*, which had by then seemed to evaporate. Jennifer already possessed a sort of parochial celebrity, one based on acquaintance rather than mediation, manipulation and illusion. She was an off-centre cynosure in whatever milieu she found herself.

In the milieu where I first encountered her there was plenty of competition. Round New Year 1967, through a friend who was going out with the elder, I was introduced to the orbit of two Persian sisters. They lived in a cramped overheated conversion in Cadogan Gardens with their mother, whose specialities were big sulks and pungent stews. They were forever trying to escape her presence and their smells, so spent much of the day walking the King's Road, hanging out in the Picasso with hirsute mutts, lunching in the Casserole with velvet mules. For their part they wore hundredweights of kohl, pioneeringly short skirts and floppy hats.

Late in January when I rang, their mother told me they had returned to school. School! That two such exotics should do something so mundane as attend school was near inconceivable. But then, as I was to discover, Padworth College was no ordinary school even if it did occupy standard-issue private educational premises, a large, dour, Georgian house near Aldermaston. Otherwise it rather broke the mould. Or, rather, if it had models they were fictional: Ronald Searle's St Trinian's and Roger Longrigg's Passion Flower Hotel. The pupils were all girls between the ages of about fifteen and nineteen, the majority of them from outside Britain. A current member of the staff told me: there is an international aspect to the college. I didn't inquire whether young male teachers are still permitted to exercise *droit de prof* over their pupils or whether the weekend curriculum still includes bacchanalian parties like those which the dumpy, distrait headmaster Peter Fison would pass through deep in conversation with Bernard Levin and quite oblivious to the drunkenness, joints, couplings and other teenage staples.

Presiding over the *ad hoc* saturnalia was the college's matron, whom, much as I enjoyed the licence of these singular events, I adjudged to be both entirely unsuitable for that post and just the matron I'd like to have had at school. Matron was Jennifer. She was imposing, boozy, brassy, bonhomous, loud and she clearly considered that keeping her charges on the straight and narrow was not part of her remit. Indeed rather the contrary. I can't have met her more than three times in her matron guise but I still wonder at the sheer improbability of her having ever obtained the post. Maybe Peter Fison had a perverse sense of humour, for Jennifer was no more interested in youth as a generality than she was in monkeys or soldiers or circus clowns: she pronounced herself uninterested in children but was captivated by my daughter Lily's precocity and Jesuitical ratiocination. She was capricious, she liked according to criteria of her own devising, according to how taken she was by an individual's quiddity. Which is not to say that she was insensitive to name or to status. But in the hermetic world of that bizarre school she didn't bother to dissemble her affections or antipathies. The very force of her presence daunted some of the girls. Others among them must have been misled into believing the notion that the English are indeed as eccentric as they are reputed to be, something which familiarity with the breed suggests is founded in national self-delusion rather than in actuality: still, if you were sent here to learn English at a country house in Berkshire and encountered Jennifer you could not but be confirmed in your prejudices.

She was welcoming and generous towards me because (a) I was voluble — I never learnt the mores of silent cool that were *de rigueur* on the King's Road and (b) I was at RADA and was green enough not to have yet begun to loathe what would, two decades later, come to be called luvviedom: I was still in thrall to the idea of acting and this rendered me an object of some fascination to Jennifer, who did not, I am pretty sure, refer to her own brief spell in the theatre but devoted herself to imagining an ideal role for me — she hit on the alluring psychopath Danny in Emlyn Williams's *Night Must Fall*. She could flatter all right.

Some time in November 1978 Terry Kilmartin, the literary editor of the *Observer*, for which paper I then worked, commissioned me to compose the Christmas quiz. No sooner had I delivered it than Terry discovered that Donald Trelford, the editor, had commissioned a quiz from Christopher Booker. I was thenceforth decommissioned and had to sell mine elsewhere. Thus I happened to be at the offices of the *Spectator* early one afternoon correcting proofs of a hundred questions and answers in a freezing room while from a floor up came the hoots and cries, burps and farts of gentlemen at lunch. At some juncture, round about the time of the tenth cognac course, one of the gentlemen remembered that a minion was slaving downstairs: Geoffrey Wheatcroft fell into the freezing room, generously banged down a couple of bottles of wine and did his level best to articulate the sentiment that these might help.

An hour or so later Jennifer processed through the door with a cup of coffee for me. We did not immediately recognize each other. She had by now achieved a semblance of the appearance that she would retain for the rest of her life. She was unimpressed that I had quit acting when I finished at RADA, even more unimpressed that I worked for the *Observer*, which she regarded with a distaste that was genuine. But that would figure, she was tolerant of most traits save priggishness: I'll never forget the face she once made, like that of the world's most sourly malevolent child, when the name of the Ur-Prig Blair was mentioned.

The yelping and whooping had rather abated: they were getting tired in the playground. Jennifer went back upstairs to egg them on in her role of anti-matron.

Jennifer was a touchline anarch who enjoyed watching others get their retaliation in first. She cut such an extraordinary figure that it was easy to overlook the fact that she was, for most of her life, a deuteragonist rather than a main player. Her wit was considerable but it was reactive rather than initiatory. Drink coarsened it, always does. But better that than periphrasis. She never stooped to euphemism. She was a bit on the truthful side for certain tastes. She didn't set out to offend, and rarely did. But she did ridicule and she did embarrass — she was more a mocker than a hater. I can think of one poor sod, an academic not so much sensitive as uptight, whose invariable reaction to Jennifer's calling a spade a spade and a fairy a faggot was to contort his face in a rictus that summoned up Edward's at Berkeley.

Just as Jennifer achieved at the age of fifty an immutable look, so did she achieve an immutable mentation and set of attitudes or affectations — there's not so much difference between the two, we grow into our affectations, it's the means by which we create ourselves. Once Jennifer had created herself she didn't tinker much with the result. The world changed around her and she eagerly neglected to keep up. She may have enjoyed stasis, may even have enjoyed presenting herself as a throwback to a golden age of her own whimsy when Mass had rhymed with arse and people still talked of receipts: these were actually a couple of affectations to which she lent such emphasis that I wonder if she ever really did grow into them.

Jennifer was usually more convincing in her locutions. *En route* to a party in Somerset I took her to meet Alan

Yentob at his medieval house outside Bridgwater. This was soon after *Two Fat Ladies* had become a hit. "Which one is she?" Alan whispered urgently as Jennifer got out of my car (which she had instructed me to drive at 100mph so that we did London to Bristol in under ninety minutes). Jennifer was taken by the place, by Philippa, by Alan. By the next time I saw her they had met on a few further occasions and they were clearly mutually appreciative (gourmand, generous, gregarious, socially adept, party-going, loquacious, etc.). She referred to him as "your nice little Jew". This would no doubt be taken by the Ur-Prig's government as further conclusive proof that the elderly are conservative and "racist" rather than as the expression of unmitigated affection it was intended to be, an expression which would have passed unnoticed by the generation Jennifer belonged to by preference if not by age.

Most people who appear on telly want to be on telly so badly that they are willing to do anything to be there; they're happy to make ingratiating berks of themselves. It was Jennifer's good fortune that she was able to give the impression that she was indifferent to what anyone thought of her, that she didn't mind whether or not she was adored. Her demeanour spelled it out: this is what you're getting, like it or lump it. This of course was merely a facet of her performance. She was as eager to be there as she was to play down that eagerness whose extent may be measured by the fact that she accepted a grotesquely paltry fee for her first series. Or maybe she simply didn't know what she should have been paid. The worldliness which informed her observation of the human circus did not extend to pecuniary affairs, her instinct for the material was not sharp. Which makes it so satisfying that she belatedly hit the jackpot — though, as I told her during the last lunch we had together a few weeks before she died, being the beneficiary of the terminal English taste for cooking as entertainment was like taking candy from babies. She grinned in cordial agreement.

Oxtail with Prunes
SERVES 6

The feast day of St George on 23 April seems to go by with hardly a whimper. I wonder why. Beloved Albion was the ancient name for the British Isles, so called because the Romans connected it with *albus*, meaning white, with reference to the chalk cliffs of Dover. Many foreign chefs have made a boo-boo using the name in describing dishes of a brown colour and it is often wrongly applied to a brown soup. The correct Albion soups include a white fish consommé thickened with tapioca and garnished with shreds of lobster or a rich white poultry potage with pea-sized balls of carrot and cucumber floating therein.

All through Lent I hanker for rich, brown oxtail, so this Easter Saturday I rushed out and bought some fine specimens and a bunch of ravishing young turnips. I concocted the dish with the addition of prunes and found it richly rewarding.

2.25-2.75kg (5-6 lb) oxtail
75g (6 oz) salt pork or unsmoked bacon
4 medium onions
4 large carrots
4 celery stalks
a bouquet of 2 bay leaves, parsley, thyme and 2 crushed
    garlic cloves
salt, pepper, mace and allspice
400g (14 oz) tin of chopped tomatoes

300ml (½ pint) Guinness or stout
275g (10 oz) prunes (ready to eat)
1 tablespoon each of Worcestershire sauce, mushroom
    ketchup and tomato purée

✳ Buy the pork or bacon in a piece, remove the rind
    and cut the meat into small dice. Chop the onions and
    slice the carrots and celery. Put the diced pork into
    the bottom of a large, heavy casserole, cover with the
    chopped vegetables and cook on a very low heat for
    about 10 minutes until the fat from the pork is
    beginning to melt and run. Arrange the pieces of
    oxtail neatly on top, enclose the bouquet garni in a
    scrap of butter muslin and plunge it into the middle.
    Season the meat with salt, pepper, mace and allspice.
    Cover the pot and cook gently for about 30 minutes.

✳ Preheat the oven to 140°C/275°F/Gas 1.

✳ Heat the tomatoes and Guinness together in a little
    saucepan until they come to the boil. Place the
    prunes on top of the oxtail and pour over the tomato
    and Guinness mixture. When the contents of the pot
    are just bubbling, cover with a sheet of foil and the
    lid, place in the oven and cook for 4 hours until the
    meat is practically falling off the bones, which is
    essential with oxtail.

✳ Using a slotted spoon, fish out the tail pieces and put
    them on a plate, then put all the juice and vegetables
    through a food mill. Return this sauce to the

casserole, add the Worcestershire sauce, the mushroom ketchup and the tomato purée. Mix thoroughly and check the seasoning. Cool, then leave in the refrigerator until the fat has risen to the top and solidified. Remove the fat and restore the pieces of oxtail to the sauce. Heat gently on top of the stove until all is mixed well together, then finish off in a low oven until piping hot.

✴ This can all take place over two days to suit your convenience. I should serve with a good potato purée and little buttered turnips with a good cutting of chives, tarragon and parsley sprinkled over them. Excellent.

"Is there any more champagne in that bottle?"

Jonathan, Jodi and Christian Routh

The temptation is to think that Jennifer just *happened* (in her case, not so much out of a genie's lamp as from a cardinal's altar bottle). There we were, my wife Nandi, sons Jodi, ten, and Christian, eight, in the dining room of our Sloane Street apartment — some time in early 1960, I would think — and so there was Jennifer, checking that the boys had bathed themselves properly before retiring to bed, and double-checking on the phone with the restaurant where we planned to have dinner. *How* was she there? *Why* was she there? Had we ever even *seen her* before? All very baffling, but after we left, when the babysitter arrived, all very entertaining. It was as though we'd known each other for years. Of course she returned to the apartment with us and indeed passed all the nights of that week and the succeeding week there. In fact, at least half of the rest of that year.

Recently I wrote to my sons asking them what they remembered of Jennifer at this time.

"Jennifer was," Christian wrote back, "a sort of nanny/ auntie/hostess/cook/spiritual teacher/social etiquette adviser to me from about the age of 8 onwards. She could also be a terrible bully, and seemed to enjoy humiliating me at the same time as she was somehow showing that she cared deeply about us. Whatever domestic turmoil or triumphs were going on she was a constant, who seemed to sort of live with us some of the time, but who was certainly there if a dinner party was going on, which was often. Her presence was never questioned; it was a given.

"She treated everyone exactly the same, be they her perennial entourage of high-ranking officers of the Catholic Church, my school-mates, dinner guests, porters, waiters, girl-friends, the rich and famous, or even our dogs: she had something to say to everyone, and would usually leave us laughing, but often feeling a bit battered by the encounter.

"Most evenings she would end up singing a song about 'Willie the Weeper' in a fearsome bass voice — unless she was with Fiore Henriques the sculptress when it would be heavy bass opera.

"And often, when most people were already drunk (though I was never sure if she was or not, her behaviour never seemed to change much), she would suddenly start honking on about St Joseph and what a 'splendid fellow' he was. Those short little sermons would be delivered with enormous gusto and faith, before she returned to the vital business of drinking."

Jennifer's presence in our house continued for a dozen years at least. And, after that house, there were other houses, not always so conveniently situated — like one in Hampshire and another in Tuscany — but never for long without Jennifer visiting them and looking as though she'd been living in them all her life. Actually, when she was with us in Sloane Street we soon discovered there was another family with whom she had a similar relationship, the Peploes, in a rather better address than ours off Belgrave Square. I think sometimes all she did on her motorcycle each day was just drive between the two of us and investigate who had the better-stocked fridge and bar.

My son Jodi writes that he remembers one particular night at Sloane Street, 23 May 1971, his twenty-first birthday. "The police had knocked at the front door, and they came up in the lift to where Jennifer opened our apartment door. They were following a complaint about rowdiness and drug abuse, they explained, from an anonymous caller. Jennifer said, 'No, we have none of that here, but do come in and have a drink.'" (Christian's version of the story has the police being met "by Jennifer and her gang of incredibly old Catholic dignitaries, most wearing dog-collars and all sipping champagne" and Jennifer bellowing, "Hello, fuzz. Have some fizz.") Back to Jodi's account: "The police entered past Jennifer, only to be greeted by Uncle Anthony and a large gent in black with a white dog-collar and little purple cap who offered the three uniformed constables a glass each and poured out three dollops of good consecrated red wine. They stood in the doorway most of the time, about fifty people moving around them in flowing kaftans. The Doors were playing loudly on the record player and Brian Auger even more loudly on his mobile organ, and Mum in the corner was busy rolling a joint. Jennifer played it so cool the police did not notice quite what was happening and with a little 'Hush, hush, off you go, and go and do something useful, please' she got rid of the cops."

Well, inevitably one thing led to another. As my *Candid Camera* programme got off the ground, I found I badly needed someone to explain to members of the public whom we'd been filming that they had just been filmed and, in return for some small sum of money, we'd like them to sign the attached form, which would give us permission to show this film. Jennifer was the obvious person for the job. So from having been in her company for maybe just half a day each day, I was now letting myself in for being with her most days twenty-four hours a day.

Nor did her job on the programme stop just at waving pieces of paper. Once we were filming in a Lyons tea-house and the person I actually wanted to involve in the film was seated at a table out of camera range. So it was quickly arranged for Jennifer to be the cleaning lady with a mop and pail on the floor just by the table of our desired person and to gradually push the table along to a position where the camera could see it. Not a very big deal, perhaps, but that day Jennifer was planning to have lunch with one of her duchesses and so had dressed for the part. Poor lady, all those beautiful clothes soaking in the dirty water on the floor.

On another occasion we were filming in Dublin Airport. The simple plot was that the plane could not accommodate overweight passengers unless they lost a little weight — to which end I, from my booking-in desk, would direct them to a corner of the airport where they could attempt to reduce their size by jumping up and down for half an hour. I was finding it quite difficult to convince some of the larger passengers booking in to adopt this course until I got Jennifer, already in the corner, jumping. Once they saw someone else was involved in this mad scene, then they were more willing to cooperate. It turned out to be just what we needed, but we omitted to tell her she could stop, so she continued jumping until we broke filming. She was not the most pleased of Jennifers at the end of that day.

Actually, I used to sack her quite often. Very rarely to do with anything she had or hadn't done. Just the amount of drink I'd had, most likely. But she was solicitous enough never to fail to turn up the following day.

I know I could not have continued with that programme as long as I did without Jennifer's help and presence. She was invaluable to me.

There are so many things I could say about her. How when I ungallantly walked out on my first wife, Nandi, the mother of my sons, Jennifer commiserated with Nandi so much and kept her sane. How when a little later Nandi died in a car accident Jennifer commiserated with me and kept me almost sane. "And you needn't go round to her apartment and look for mementoes amongst her clothes," she admonished me. "Uncle Anthony and I have been round and taken them all — twenty-five cases of them — and they're now hanging in Westminster Cathedral at a vantage point where the poor of Pimlico can help themselves to them." How could I complain? And then, every now and then in her conversation, there'd be tantalizing hints about her past — "When I was in Shanghai" or "When I was cooking in Tripoli" — on which she'd never expand. But I saw her in action as matron of a young ladies' finishing school near Reading adding measures of gin to the medicines she offered sickly girls, so why shouldn't she have been a cook in Tripoli?

"Your programme," she said to me many years later, "simply turned you into a TV personality. But mine, mine has made me a cult figure — whatever that may be — but you can be sure there aren't many of us around. And you should be very honoured one's talking to you now."

"I am Jennifer, I am. Deeply so," I said.

Jodi's account of Jennifer to me ends: "Sonja, my wife, and I were staying with Christian in north London as the tabloid headlines about Jennifer being diagnosed with advanced cancer lay across the breakfast table. Holding a big sunflower and a bottle of champagne with some Carr's cheese biscuits, we got through the cordon of security at the Westminster Hospital and presented ourselves to the ward matron. We were asked to leave the mascarpone cheese and all would be OK. It took some convincing that we were not delivering for a Chelsea delicatessen but in actual fact were the real likely lads. Her room was full of postcards, packets, bottles of champagne and a little Italian trying to stuff a far too small fridge with about ten packets of mascarpone. After we had finished with the where, what and why interrogation from Jennifer (she was visibly pleased to see us), she was obviously at an end, but making jokes all the way — 'I died last Friday you know,' she exclaimed. 'But I resurrected the next morning — is there any more champagne in that bottle?' When we left, my wife Sonja was waiting for me in the hospital foyer, she held me as I collapsed and cried."

I would have done the same.

It still worries me that, just because I was laid up in a Tuscan hospital with some totally curable disease, I never got to the bedside, or even to the funeral. I know, once, she would have forgiven me, but it's too late now. So, a guilty conscience for the rest of my life. Serves me right.

Oh, Jennifer, I do so miss you. Please, just *happen* again somewhere.

Potatoes Ruspoli
SERVES 4-6

A few years ago I visited Tuscany, in the midst of the Chianti Classico country where I stayed with my old *Candid Camera* mate Jonathan Routh and his wife Shelagh. While we all know quite a bit about Tuscan food by now, we may forget the wonderful natural produce out there: the gorgeous gnarled tomatoes; the buffalo mozzarella, figs, pears, peppers and cheeses which really taste; whole, stuffed, roasted pigs in the market; grilled pigeons of melting tenderness and vast veal chops all cooked on the charcoal fires. While we were there, I had a very good Italian lunch at the house of Julio Ruspoli who produces a very excellent Chianti Classico red which we imbibed. The lunch was delicious but the dish that caught my fancy was an unusual potato mixture.

750g (1½ lb) potatoes
2 large yellow pimentos
2 good-sized onions
3 tablespoons olive oil
300ml (½ pint) good stock, warmed
salt
freshly ground pepper
chopped parsley

✻ Use new or waxy potatoes that will not dwindle into a mush. Scrub or scrape them and cut into smallish chunks. De-seed the pimentos, cut away the pith and slice fairly thickly into diamond shapes. Chop up the onions and fry gently in the olive oil until soft. Add the potatoes and the pimentos, mix well with the onions, then pour in half the warmed stock. Cook until tender, uncovered, adding more stock if necessary (I used the full 300ml/½ pint).

✻ When ready, season with salt and freshly ground pepper and sprinkle with a good handful of chopped parsley. Serve with any meat, poultry or fish dish. It is also very good when cold as a salad.

Jennifer in Print

Tom Hartman
Anthony Blond
Charles Moore
Peter Ackroyd
Clare Asquith

The siren song of the press is heard. Tom Hartman, publisher and famous coiner of puns, reminds us that Jennifer's first appearance in print was as the stand-in on the *Evening Standard*. But that was a mere prelude to the period of her life when she became a "figure", the *Spectator* years. We are reminded of crashing crockery, pulsating motorbikes, and bad behaviour. Anthony Blond, the writer and former publisher; Charles Moore, now editor of the *Daily Telegraph* and future chosen biographer of Margaret Thatcher; Peter Ackroyd, who was one of the *Spectator*'s literary editors, but is better known for his prize-winning biographies of Eliot, Blake, Dickens and Thomas More, and a considerable list of fine novels; Clare Asquith, vividly representing the magazine's engine room . . . together they conjure up a

58

sparkling — often literally — picture of a great eccentric emerging from her chrysalis and flying about to general delight and some nervousness on the part of her observers.

Lady Macbeth's Friend

Tom Hartman

Jennifer and I first met some time in the late 1950s. Neither of us could remember in later years exactly where or when, but we think that it was probably at a party given by a rather splendid lady called Diana Carter Campbell. I say "splendid" because Diana had that wonderful ability to rise above economic handicaps and somehow always keep the drinks tray full without any apparent means of financial support. Jennifer said that Diana made me read an extract from *The Little Prince*. Of this I have no recollection, but, on whatever occasion it was, we instantly became firm friends.

I think at that time she was working in the Complaints Department at Harrods. I remember wondering what sort of reception the complainants got. In those days my father was still alive and my family home was virtually out of bounds as he was usually drunk and guests were not welcomed. He died in 1963 and the following year I took Jennifer down to Almeley, my mother's house in Herefordshire. It must have been at about one in the morning when we arrived. "We'll go in through the back," I said, "as Mamma will have gone to bed." She had, but she heard the car and as we came into the hall from the back of the house she appeared in her nightdress at the top of the stairs. "My god, it's Lady Macbeth," said Jennifer and from that moment on they became the best of friends. The visitors' book, which survives, tells me that she came down fourteen times in the five years before my mother died. On one occasion she brought Jonathan and Nandi Routh; it was with the former that she had worked on the TV show *Candid Camera*. Jonathan reintroduced the inhabitants of the village to the forgotten medieval pastime of egg-rolling, which simply meant rolling hard-boiled eggs down the rather steep village street. It was hardly surprising that it had been "forgotten" since Jonathan had invented it on the spur of the moment.

After my mother died I was obliged to sell the house and we had a big farewell party which coincided with the christening of my daughter Sophie, Jennifer's god-daughter. We had about sixteen people for lunch, most of the village for tea and buns after the christening and a big party for about sixty of the local *gratin* in the evening. Jennifer, ably assisted by my late mother's loyal staff Sheila and Mrs Welsh, did all the catering. I can still see her wandering around with a mixing bowl in her hand, saying, "Don't worry, my darling. It will all be all right."

The christening itself was not without incident. The vicar says to Jennifer, holding the baby, "What name do you give this child?" or words to that effect, to which Jennifer replies, "Hilaria Munga", those being her feminized version of the saints for the day on which Sophie was born. Thereupon Allan Peile, her godfather, snatched the baby from Jennifer's arms and said, "No, no, Lucy Sophia!" Jennifer told me that she had had to get permission from the cardinal of the day to act as godmother to a child baptized in the Anglican Church. She was always one for going straight to the top. She once introduced me to Cardinal Hume and told him that I was a passionate fisherman, which was totally untrue. He took me to his bookshelf of fishing books and pointed to his favourite work: it had been written by my Uncle Bobby, which got me out of an awkward situation.

Christmas was part of the routine. For over twenty years Jennifer came to lunch with us at my house in Battersea on Christmas Day. For this my children had to be well prepared, for she was not one to mince her words. I would buy them presents to give to her but I had to warn them that the possible response might be, "Oh well, I suppose I can hand it on to someone some time." She told me that she had a special drawer in which she put what she called "Passover Presents".

Some time in the late 1980s, not long after my wife left, Jennifer said to me, "Will you come up to Cumberland with me? I get so bored there on my own." It transpired that she spent a week there every summer with a friend of hers called Patricius Senhouse. I said that I'd never met him. She said that didn't matter, we'd soon be friends, and so we set off together. I shall never forget our lunch *en route*. We stopped at some dreadful motorway burger joint which had tables and chairs in the garden. Jennifer then produced a white tablecloth, quails' eggs, cold grouse, white wine, red wine, etc.,

etc., and people gathered around us looking in amazement. "You silly fools," said Jennifer, "there's no need to go in there and buy that filth."

We drove on and finally reached Cockermouth, to be welcomed by Mr Senhouse, for the first of about eight annual visits. The routine was much the same every year: out to lunch, back to supper and old films on the video in the evening. But what lunches! Invariably we would go to Ela and Charlie Carlisle at Naworth Castle, then to lovely Annie Liddle, whose dogs Jennifer hated, then to Tommy Bates, who poured incredibly strong drinks and whose chum Jane Torday combined wit and attraction to an enviable degree. There was also Mrs Lowther, who I think came from California, but we had much to thank her for for not having stayed there. If ever there was a life-enhancer it was, and I hope still is, Mrs Lowther. Another port of call was the house of Mr and Mrs Ian Lowe, where the drink and the conversation flowed with equal liberality.

I think I can claim without undue unmodesty that I had some hand in launching Jennifer on the road to fame. Shortly after Geoffrey Wheatcroft, whom I had known when we worked together at Hamish Hamilton, was made literary editor of the *Spectator* he asked me out to lunch, which was in itself an unusual occurrence. He told me that Alexander Chancellor, then the sainted editor, was planning to give a weekly luncheon party. Did I know anyone who would do the cooking? Immediately I suggested Jennifer and she got the job. The cooking led to the cookery column and so on.

Anthony Blond had the idea of publishing her receipts, as Jennifer called them, as a book. He put the idea to Naim Attallah in a memo which said something like: "She is a spinster with no knowledge of the finances of the book world so we should get it cheap." Unfortunately the memo was put in the wrong envelope and sent to Jennifer. We were off the next day to Cumbria, where Patricius was giving a big party to celebrate his sixtieth birthday, to which Anthony had also been invited. Jennifer showed him the memo, by which he was in no way abashed. Indeed I have never seen that most loveable of men abashed. In his memoirs, yet to be published, Anthony describes me as "eximious". I think that the word applies more accurately both to him and to Jennifer.

In the end Jennifer's book was published by the eminent house of John Murray. They gave a launching party to which Jennifer insisted that I should come with her, not merely just to be there but to hold her hand from the start. We were greeted by the publicity manager or some such and Jennifer was shown where she could sign copies and so forth. After a while she said to me, pointing to a small man with a white cloth over his arm, "I'm worried about that waiter. I think he's drunk." "Don't be a fool," I said, "that's Jock Murray sending you up!"

As a result of the cookery column Jennifer was asked to stand in at one point for the restaurant correspondent for the *Evening Standard*, who had taken a year's sabbatical. I think it may have been Nigella Lawson. Jennifer frequently asked me to accompany her on these outings and invariably mentioned my name in her subsequent reports, on one occasion referring to me as "the Old Etonian dwarf". One night we were told to go to a place called School Dinners, where the clientele seemed to be mostly of what is now called "estuarine" origin. The gimmick was that the waitresses were skimpily dressed as schoolgirls, people got up and said, "I've been a naughty boy" and were then hauled up on to a stage and caned by one of the girls. I said to Jennifer, "At my prep school they did that on one's bare bum," whereupon the man bending over on the stage took his trousers and pants down, almost as if he had heard me. Jennifer, a true puritan at heart, was appalled. She mentioned the incident in her article, as a result of which the place was besieged by photographers.

After *Two Fat Ladies* started I saw less of her, we having met, I suppose, at least once a week for the past thirty years. I once said to Patricia Llewellyn, the inventor and producer of the programme, how wonderful it was for Jennifer, never having had any money all her life, suddenly to be really quite rich, to which Patricia replied, "Yes, but I wish she'd sometimes buy the crew a round of drinks." The problem was that Jennifer had never had what one might call spare cash and when it came her way she simply didn't know what to do with it. She came round for a drink one evening when the *Fat Ladies* was well established and asked if she could stay for supper. I don't keep food in the house, so I said I'd send out for a "Chinese". "Wonderful," she said, "I've never had a Chinese takeaway before." I gave her the menu, which I keep by the telephone. She wanted about five or six dishes. "That's enough for about eight people," I said, "and it is quite expensive." "Darling," she replied, "I've never had Chinese before and I want to try them all." Pulling out her purse, she thrust a fistful of notes into my hand and said, "You see, I've got all this money and I really don't know what to do with it, so you just spend it."

Sophie and I visited her a number of times in hospital in the weeks before she died. On one occasion a doctor was in the room. "Do you want us to go away?" I asked Jennifer. "Not at all," she answered. "This is Dr Death. He has come to tell me that I am dying and he thinks I ought to be upset. I can't think why. I knew it already and I'm quite ready to meet my Maker." To which I could only reply, "Yes, darling, but is He ready to meet you?" I hope He was.

For over forty years Jennifer enriched my life far more than any words can convey. Our love for each other, purely platonic as it was, is something which I will always cherish.

Crab au Gratin
SERVES 4

As a cure for my foot warts, I am having to bind each toe in fresh banana skins every day, so I have been trying to find ways of using the fruit as I don't particularly like a plain banana, or even one with cream as did that naughty father of Auberon Waugh. One method I have found palatable is to cover them in a lime and oil vinaigrette with the addition of a lot of Worcestershire sauce, rather as though they were avocados. This also went very well with a fish curry. The following receipt is another good way of using them up.

1 good tablespoon butter
1 good tablespoon plain flour
300ml (½ pint) single cream
75g (3 oz) freshly grated Parmesan cheese
salt
freshly ground black pepper
Tabasco
grated nutmeg (optional)
50ml (2 fluid oz) medium sherry
450g (1 lb) crab meat (brown and white)
anchovy essence
4 tablespoons fresh breadcrumbs
extra butter
4 bananas

✳ Make a béchamel sauce by combining the butter and flour in a pan and cooking gently for a couple of minutes; then stir in the cream, a little at a time, and increase the heat until the sauce thickens. When ready stir in most of the cheese, reserving some for sprinkling later. When it is mixed and melted, season well with the salt and pepper and a good dash or so of Tabasco and maybe a little grated nutmeg. Add the sherry, then stir in the crab meat, adding a little anchovy essence to suit your taste. Put the mixture into a shallow gratin dish.

✳ Mix the breadcrumbs with the remaining cheese and sprinkle all over the top. Dot with butter and grill until nice and brown.

✳ Peel the bananas, cut them in half lengthways and fry in 40g (1½ oz) of butter. Serve with the crab.

The Queeny End of the Market

Anthony Blond

She was a legend to her friends before becoming legendary to millions. In Britain, even in North America, Australia and Japan, the fat lady was triumphant but she had not needed to arrange her act for the telly. Her hoots, her puckered mouth when doubting, her Woodbine wheezes, her Hanoverian laughter, her one-liners which grew riper with age and fame — "Darling, I've had more faggots at my feet than Joan of Arc" — were privately famous before she went public. Her roaring joy in life, her gusto, her reminiscence, the overflow of a well-stocked mind, her operatic outbursts and, let us not forget, her cooking, were relished by an immense number of friends whom she enlivened (and infuriated) and, a good Catholic lady, when in distress, succoured.

Her flip side showed of course when she was "emotional" but never tired with it, and all of us must have vowed, at some time, never to see Jennifer again — at least for a week — for she could be cruelly rude and in these moods did not suffer even intelligent people gladly. But firing Jennifer, as Charles Moore had said, had no effect. The bullets turned into marshmallows.

Jennifer's translation — it was not a transformation — to fame and fortune was like a cinematic cut. Think of the opening of the second half of *Dr Zhivago* when Tom Courtenay, last seen as a ranting student in a café, appears as a commissar in the sitting room of his own train; apropos that film, when unable to sleep, because I had forgotten the theme tune, I rang Jennifer, who delivered without demur. She was never discomposed, except on her own initiative.

Jennifer's talent to amuse was not distorted by exposure to millions, nor did the money it brought her affect her *train de vie*. She, who knew everybody, was suddenly someone whom everybody wanted to know. At a party given by Shoura Shihwarg, an Oxford friend of forty years' standing, Jennifer was mobbed by people she had known all her life. She was enjoying herself and only showed her new status by stuffing with maximum indiscretion a cheque for £50,000-odd into her ancient handbag, to mix with the Woodbines — she, the cathedral mouse who had never had, formerly, so many pence.

Jennifer, who had bathed for so many years — one hot night quite literally — in a bathful of the champagne of others, never knew that money could flow both ways; her television producer told me she never once offered to pay for a round of drinks for the crew. She was not mean but spending was not a concept she entertained.

This occasion was her apotheosis, for nobody knew she had not long to live.

I can't remember a time in my adult life when I did not know Jennifer. I must have met her at Oxford in 1948 in the glorious company of Milo Cripps, a fellow Catholic, whose mother, the Hon. Mrs Freddy, had been a Duchess of Westminster and lived in a large and gloomy grace and favour house in South Audley Street, later moving to Eaton Square, where Jennifer became her *dame de compagnie* for a time, and her rôle model for all time. Here are two of her favourite stories. Driving down the King's Road, Violet, swerving past a black man on a bicycle: "Times have changed, knock a Negro over on his bike in your Bentley and you've had it"; and, reading about the emergence of the coelacanth: "Been there at the bottom of the ocean for a million years and now it turns up, bold as brass!"

Although not "up" at Oxford, Jennifer easily matched the loquacity, the showiness, the snobbery (I fear) of the party-going set within the class of '48. We admired the exhibitionism and wit of Kenneth Peacock Tynan, who had avoided conscription by affecting homosexuality. We were more oriented to what was not yet known as the media than to politics. I did not shine at the Union, whose then President, Godfrey Smith, became an up-to-a-point-Lord-Copper secretary to Lord Kemsley at the *Sunday Times*, where he still functions. Among our lot were Robert Robinson, Robin Day, Paul Johnson, who harboured Jimmy Goldsmith when he was on the run, and Michael Codron. Nobody ever knew what would become of Alan Clark, finally better known for his scandalous diaries than for his achievements as a Tory Minister. These were solid citizens compared to the frothy, gamy Peter Fison, whose gourmandizing was caricatured by Michael Rutherston, a reincarnation of

Max Beerbohm and the first young man I knew to die of a broken heart. Supported by Milo, Peter started a sort of "Dothegels Hall", a boarding school for the difficult and high-spirited daughters of London diplomats, where he employed Jennifer as matron. The catering allowance was parsimonious and Jennifer coped by feeding the gels from tins of raspberry jam sluiced down with gallons of cheap cider, so that they went squiffy to bed and too tired to try to escape. Michael Molian, who we all thought was a genius but through some error by the university authorities was awarded a third-class honours degree, was offered by Peter the post of "unpaid manciple", which he declined in preference to a job in UNESCO.

Milo had acquired a large, very non-Regency house on the sea front in Hove which for some reason Jennifer called "Garth". It became a weekend colony for private spirited friends like Molian, who lived nearby with his Jewish mother, who spoilt him rotten, so that when he came to stay the night in Chester Row and I brought him tea at six o'clock in the morning to wake him for his train to Paris from Victoria, he thought nothing of it. However, when he reached Paris I did get a reward, in the form of a bread-and-butter postcard. He admired naval and military personnel — and it read: "On returning to Paris I found that my office had been moved to a position overlooking, as I am unable to do, the playing fields of the Champs de Mars."

Jennifer collected exotic persons at the queeny end of the market — Truman Capote being a typical catch — but was herself a collectors' item, never without a glass or two (or ten) of champagne in the hand. But she was generous in sharing with her low-flying friends her high-flying connections. She did not neglect the former and did not exploit the latter. The idea of quid pro quo, or cutlet for cutlet, was irrelevant; so, not a child of her times, but then of whose times was she a child? Perhaps of the eighteenth century as the abbess of a nunnery whose walls the young Talleyrand found it easy to scale; or, again in France, with a salon like Madame du Deffand's, for I can hear her saying, "Talk more loudly, my dears, for I am about to pass wind."

With her sharp, Catholic morality and her loud voice Jennifer could have become the governor of a women's prison, but though she had the style and temper to sustain any of these professions she lacked the will and the ambition, for her curriculum vitae was a maze of zigzags, without ups or downs as in snakes and ladders, until that splendid, almost accidental late flowering, which turned her into an international telly star.

Before that, Jennifer had edited magazines for Norman Kark, who derived his main income from a large neon sign in Trafalgar Square, where she worked, had nannied rich children, been girl Friday to Jonathan Routh's *Candid Camera* — much funnier and quite cruel, an element I fancy Jennifer enjoyed, on the radio — at the same time organizing life for his mistress, the Dutch Shell heiress Olga Deterding, who terminated their affair by emptying his wardrobe down the lift shaft of the building in Piccadilly where she had a penthouse, complete with flagpole, and where in 1978 she gave me a launch party for my novel *Family Business*. Some of these employments were quite short and not sweet at all. Typical, often quoted, was her stint as housekeeper to a Nigerian diplomat in a mansion flat near the Albert Hall. Jennifer refused to draw his bedroom curtains in the morning for fear of encountering "any piece of white trash" he might have dragged back, so she stood outside his door and bellowed: "Your eggy's ready now, Mr Ruanda."

Always Jennifer was a cook. I sold my house in Doughty Street to the *Spectator* in the early 1970s and the top floor became a kitchen and dining room where Jennifer famously performed. But she still came to Chester Row whenever I had a dinner party. She arrived on her scooter with the food and bits of her own *batterie de cuisine* and descended to the basement, where the statutory bottle of whisky awaited her. Then she began to sing. Her arias flowed upwards and we knew all was well. She and a sculptress, an androgynous figure credited with carrying a Jew under each arm over the Alps to safety before the war, made two good bass ladies, rattling the teaspoons.

Finally she donned the historic helmet, the brilliants of the eyebrows glittering in the street lamps of lower Belgravia and chuntered home, always safely, to her insalubrious quarters in the shadow of Westminster Cathedral and so to bed, praying, but not exclusively, for the death of her mother. The apartment, which never saw the sun, was shabby and not really big enough for her mother, who did eventually oblige her by dying, and her uncle, a dealer in Catholic paraphernalia and an expert on liturgy who endured her abuse, which increased as she lay vociferously dying, surrounded by caviare and champagne, with a patience rare among the saints she constantly invoked. Apart from her other Jesuit uncle, who ran a nest of priests in Golden Lane, whom she admired, Jennifer's relations with her family who, she imagined falsely, had deprived her of higher education, were unhappy; and, though she insisted on staying with her brothers and their children in the country, these visits were always fraught and painful. This aspect of her life was not visible to her friends, for whom her presence was mostly pleasurable.

Many know how to give but Jennifer was mistress in the art of receiving with grace and she was often invited on holidays. Andrew McCall and I had asked her to join a house party in the villa we had rebuilt in the middle of Corfu, on a hill overlooking the Livadhi Ropa, all expenses paid, in return for her doing the cooking. She knew Andrew well and the story goes that on meeting him one day in the King's Road, wearing "the sack", briefly fashionable but suiting her, Andrew complained her bum was too wobbly: "It should be taut, like mine," to which Jennifer replied, "Yes, but who taught it?"

To avoid a coagulation of cars by the house, spoiling the view, we had built a long, winding staircase of stone through the olive grove. On the first day Jennifer slipped, sprained her ankle, and was confined to bed, so we served *her* meals, instead of vice versa, as planned. To encourage our ministrations Jennifer admitted she had brought some American Express traveller's cheques with which she would treat us, on her recovery, to a posh meal at the Corfu Palace Hotel. Then she announced she felt strong enough to accompany us to the beach for a paddle. Clutching her handbag — for one could not trust the Greeks (the beach was empty) — she advanced into the water and, turning to acknowledge the plaudits of our crowd with a wave of her hand, she slipped again and fell into a few inches of the Ionian sea. It was enough.

Now American Express thinks of everything. Every now and again in the history of aviation a passenger aircraft plunges into the ocean with no survivors. Supposing some bodies containing wallets or purses and traveller's cheques float ashore to an island in the South Pacific and are found by fishermen, who, like the Cornish and the inhabitants of Sark, have a prayer for such events to occur, and try to cash the cheques — well, they will be foiled, because, as happened with Jennifer's, on contact with water they display ineluctably the letters "VOID".

P.S. I did not discover Jennifer but I did recognize her potential as an earner, having written to Naim Attallah, when I was advising him about books, that he should contract her because she could become a star, but at present, "being a poor Catholic spinster of this parish [Westminster] she would come cheap". Inadvertently (perhaps because my assistant Jubby, daughter of Richard Ingrams, was quite a tease) a copy of this memo was sent to Jennifer. She rang up gaily and said she had found in John Murray a much better publisher, so thanks very much. The rest is her story, in which, alas, I played no part.

Upside-down Pear Pudding
SERVES 8-10

I went to a terrific lunch at the Four Seasons Hotel, Park Lane, where the Earl and Countess of Carnarvon were presiding and Mark Greenfield, the Highclere Castle chef, was cooking dishes from their second book of receipts. Everything was delicious so I thought to include a pudding from the book.

FOR THE BASE:
225g (8 oz) soft brown sugar
100g (4 oz) butter

FOR THE CONTENTS:
4 ripe pears, peeled, cored and quartered
225g (8 oz) plain flour plus 1 teaspoon bicarbonate of soda
½ teaspoon salt
4 teaspoons cinnamon
2 teaspoons ground ginger
½ teaspoon grated nutmeg
pinch ground cloves
2 eggs, beaten
175g (6 oz) black treacle
250ml (8 fluid oz) milk
225g (8 oz) butter, melted

✳ Preheat the oven to 180°C/350°F/Gas 4.

✳ To make the base, place the sugar and butter in a saucepan over a low heat. Once melted, turn up the heat and allow to bubble for a couple of minutes. Pour into a 25cm (10 inch) oven-proof dish. Arrange the pears rounded side down on the bottom of the dish.

✳ Thoroughly mix the rest of the ingredients together and pour over the pears. Bake for one hour in the lower section of the oven.

✳ Test with a sharp, pointed knife which should come out clean; if it has raw mix sticking to it, the pudding will need further cooking. Allow to cool slightly before turning it out carefully onto some gorgeous serving plate. Eat with lightly whipped double cream or some very good vanilla ice-cream. The black treacle is the inspired ingredient, I think.

The Fat Lady Sings

Charles Moore

One summer afternoon I was sitting in the garden of the *Spectator* when the sash from the top-floor kitchen shot up and Jennifer Paterson stuck her head out. "Who's this Digby Anderson?" she yelled, brandishing the latest issue. I explained that he was to be our monthly food writer (at that time the *Spectator* did not run regular articles about cooking). "If he can do it, why can't I?" shouted Jennifer. As was often the case in conversation with Jennifer, I could not think of a riposte to trump her, so I offered her a post.

Thus began, in her seventh decade, her rise from drudge in the kitchen to fame and fortune as a television cook. She died better known than anyone else associated with the *Spectator* in modern times.

Jennifer was appointed cook at the *Spectator* by Alexander Chancellor. He later made her office manager as well, which meant taking messages on her 50cc motorbike. Alexander thought it also meant replacing the light bulb on his desk lamp, but Jennifer disagreed and he remained in darkness for many months. She disliked any change, and when we finally had the decrepit office redecorated she screamed, "The place looks like a cat-house."

If you valued what is now called your private space, Jennifer was not the person for you. She would enter any office at any time saying anything that came into her head. In the mid-1980s the paper was bought by Australians, and I was having my first, rather tense intercontinental telephone conversation with them when Jennifer barged in and started ruffling my hair, bellowing, "Darling little Editor" and smothering me with kisses. At the lunches which she cooked for the paper's guests, she would intrude her person and her thoughts upon all comers. Once, during a quarrel with Alexander, she came in and collected the remains of the first course. "That was delicious, Jennifer," he said, anxious to make peace. "What was it cooked in?" "Vitriol!"

Her television fame was particularly deserved and appreciated because she was a natural and, until then, frustrated actress. She loved singing and doing accents and striking poses. Before a big event she would have the equivalent of stage fright. Once the Prince of Wales came to lunch and the palace let us know in advance that he did not like red meat. "That bloody fusspot Prince will have whatever I give him," she said. "Your inviting him has given me a rash all up my leg." (Here she offered to show me.) But when he did come she was charm itself and the food was halibut ceviche. He and she later became friends, and he sent a letter to her hospital bed that touched her very much.

In all Jennifer's writing, the words came just as she spoke them — clear, funny, idiosyncratic. And the receipts (never say recipes) were excellent, so long as you made allowances for a certain carelessness. Some will remember the walnut and coffee cake introduced with the words "Here is a delicious and strange cake", in which she forgot to include the walnuts. I believe there was also a dish which required boiling a can of condensed milk: many readers wrote in to say that they had been injured in the resulting explosion.

One day I was sitting in my office on the first floor when I heard a great commotion and swearing from the top of the house. People came rushing down the stairs saying, "Jennifer's thrown all the coffee cups out of the window." She soon followed and, when I challenged her, she said, "Yes, the dirty mugs belonging to all those ghastly common people in advertising cluttering up my kitchen. I threw them all out." I sacked her on the spot ("I can't wait to get out"), and we went in search of the mugs. At first we could not find them, and I began to think that Jennifer was mad as well as furious, and hadn't really thrown them out at all. Eventually we realized that she had taken careful aim and chucked them into the garden of the National Association of Funeral Directors next door. After about two weeks she started coming in again, and after a month I formally reinstated her.

Three weeks ago I went to see Jennifer in hospital, but was told by serious-looking nurses that she was not well enough for visitors. Ten days later I did see her, and explained that I'd been before. "Ah yes, that was when I died," she said. She was drinking vodka, and I said it was nice the nurses let her. "I can do anything I like: I'm dying!" She had hundreds of kind letters and presents of caviare (requested in preference to chocolate), but there was one letter from a man who said her illness was her own fault for smoking. "I've written back to him and said, 'I'm 71, and you're a prat.'"

She was very brave when she was dying. This was partly because the actress in her was determined to put on a good show, and partly because her Catholic faith was her strongest characteristic. Although she was noisy about her Catholicism — as about almost everything — Jennifer was unselfconscious about it. To her it was absolutely real, so that there was no point in arguing. Like all religious people, she wove her faith into her routine, making spiritual food as necessary as physical. The saints were like friends: she knew them, loved them, conversed with them and even argued with them. Her life was fully peopled by the dead as well as the living.

If she's right, she's in Purgatory now. I think of her pulling her bad leg painfully upstairs, complaining noisily as she approaches the heavenly banquet.

A Royal Manner

Peter Ackroyd

Jennifer Paterson would have made a wonderful leader, whether religious or military. If circumstances had been more favourable, there is no doubt that she would have risen to the rank of archbishop or even cardinal; her piety was never for a moment in doubt, and indeed she practised the rituals of the Catholic Church with a fervour worthy of Ronald Firbank's ecclesiastics, and her somewhat rebarbative opinions on matters of sexual morality were often loudly expressed in the most apparently inhibiting circumstances. I have heard her hiss "Adulterer!" at a perfectly respectable person.

As a leader of men she would have enjoyed equal success. She would have been marvellous upon a field of battle, as anyone will testify who saw her screeching down the narrow thoroughfares of London on a tiny motorcycle wearing a spangled helmet crowned by a peacock's feather. She looked rather like a Christmas tree travelling over the speed limit. Here was the spirit of Boadicea or of Elizabeth, miraculously restored in the late twentieth century. I do not believe that she would have quailed at the thought of bloodshed or mass slaughter; being herself of such unusual temperament and character, she was somewhat dismissive of ordinary human complaints and human failings.

My tiny office was situated beside her kitchen, at the top of the house in Doughty Street from which the *Spectator* magazine was edited, and we enjoyed a blissful camaraderie interrupted only on those occasions when she discovered a missing morsel of cheese or a piece of pickle which in my need I had surreptitiously eaten. Then there would emerge from her kitchen — I might almost say, her cave — a human sound almost unutterable in its pain and intensity. But generally we "rubbed on" well enough — "rubbed" being perhaps the appropriate word since her large girth left little room in the narrow corridors or staircases for those of normal figure to proceed. I seem to remember that our time was spent in comments upon *Spectator* staff and guests, followed by screams of wild laughter as if we were the last two banshees left in the world. "Look at that dirty old man down there," she would say, peering into the back garden some floors below, "I know what he wants. But" — and here she would slip into a kind of sub-American voice — "he ain't gonna get it, kid." There would be occasional fits of the giggles, at a more than usually absurd remark passed at the table by a politician or other worthy; the remark would then enter our repertoire for several days, each time producing more giggles.

I recall one occasion when I had to host a lunch for the Israeli ambassador, for whom she promptly served pork. He made a polite complaint, and his plate was snatched away — to be replaced by something green and innocuous. "How was I supposed to know?" was all she said of the incident. As far as I remember she was sacked on several occasions, but returned the following morning apparently not at all the worse for the experience — in fact, rather buoyed up by it, as if she had somehow proved her mettle.

Her relationship to homosexuals was a matter of fascinated speculation among her friends. She got on with them very well — it was she who, many dark years ago, first introduced me to Quentin Crisp, who became a close friend — despite the fact that she would suddenly bellow out, "You dreadful old poof!" at fair-haired gentlemen attending normally sedate publishers' parties. They tended to treat her as a kind of *monstre sacré*, which is French for "fag hag", and she treated them with a mixture of condescension and fascination. I don't think she was herself of a sexual type — and it is still hard to think of any suitable partner for her after the bedroom door was closed — and so she felt more at ease with men who had absolutely no designs upon anything other than her lipstick case.

She could be extremely rude to those whom she considered bland or dull. "What is that dreadful man doing here?" she once inquired of a distinguished architect in a very loud — rather, an extremely loud — voice. But somehow the weight and majesty of her presence seemed to forestall any furious ripostes. I do not recall any occasion when she was answered back in kind, although of course there was no "kind" which could possibly resemble her. This tendency to a royal manner was distinctly encouraged by her latter-day success as a television presenter. Alas, I never watched any of the programmes — on what seemed to be the justifiable ground that I had seen quite enough of her in real life already — but my friends soon confirmed my abiding suspicion that she was actually better on the small screen than in the drawing room. In the presence of others she could be overbearing and difficult; in front of the cameras she seems to have emerged as a rather engaging eccentric. In the latter instances the voice, of course, could always be modified by a button. Yet I miss her. It can be said of few people that they contribute to the distinct gaiety of life; Jennifer Paterson was one such.

Thanks to
St Christopher

Clare Asquith

"The coffee comes from Bleeding Heart Yard; whisky from Unwins, for Kingsley Amis. And there's one person you *must* look out for," said my cousin Henrietta when, following in her footsteps, I was taken on in a "general capacity" by the then editor of the *Spectator*, Alexander Chancellor, in the late 1970s. "Jennifer Paterson. She's the cook there, and a wonderful character, very flamboyant. You really should make friends with her."

It was excellent advice, even if one didn't exactly have to look out for Jennifer. The following week a booming "Hello, darlings!" to no one in particular preceded a "very unusual" figure in waterproofs, scarlet lipstick, Hermès scarf beneath diamanté crash helmet, laden with food and kitchen paraphernalia, so I presented myself. "Are you Jennifer?" I asked shyly. "Yes, dear. Who are you? I don't think I've seen you before." It was a characteristic opening, direct. Dispensing with formalities. "Oh really?" she said next. "Which Asquiths are you? Are you the Mells ones?"

In fact there was a chance connection. Friends of hers had taken Mells, our family house in Somerset, on a long lease in the 1960s while we were abroad, and she had stayed there. Later we persuaded her back a few times, although she was generally unhappy in the country, where she felt stuck, and ill, among too many insects; but at least there was good bathing near by — a vast, disused limestone quarry full of clear spring water, which she loved. "I'm a mermaid, I cannot walk on land," she would exclaim, after a bizarre, experimental operation had put metal rods in her feet, the unfairytale equivalent of walking on knives — a characteristically ironic, though touching self-image.

From that moment in the hall at the *Spectator* I think she decided to take me under her wing. I had recently moved to London and didn't know many people, and was immediately grateful for her boisterous, reassuring presence. Not that the atmosphere at Doughty Street was in any way daunting; in fact it was the opposite — happy, relaxed and unstuffy, and I couldn't believe my luck to be working there. "How long would you want me for?" I'd asked Alexander anxiously, desperate for a secure job after a succession of temporary ones. "As long as you feel like staying," he'd replied, in his charming, easygoing way, which he shared in common with the owner, Henry Keswick.

We were a small staff in those days, and contributors delivered their own copy (or sometimes Jennifer collected it on her motorbike), so one soon got to know the regulars, and it had the feeling of being a large family, which I suppose most magazines had at the time, though it was all new to me. I progressed from running errands to helping on the back half of the paper, edited single-handedly by Geoffrey Wheatcroft, and even sold some classified advertising, a proud moment. And most of the staff doubled up in a "general capacity"; the managing editor read the paper for libel, the assistant editor wrote the film reviews, Alexander the diary and Geoffrey seemed to be able to write about anything, while Jenny Naipaul, Alexander's secretary, ran the place.

It was an atmosphere that suited Jennifer perfectly, where she was free to come and go as she pleased, and in fact her association with the building predated ours. Her friend, the publisher Anthony Blond, had had his offices there, and she had helped with his parties, supervising whole boar roasting on spits in the garden before most of us had known it. She liked being around an office — provided it was relaxed — and liked the idea of "workmates", even if her presence tended to inhibit any work getting done. "This is Clare, she's my mucker," was how she often introduced me. Though employed to cook the weekly lunches, she was there much more often than that, taking care of us all, or at any rate dispensing hot, neat gin for minor ailments, mainly to the girls. At one stage she suggested becoming the office manager, a position that hadn't hitherto existed, at another "official" motorbike courier, though she wasn't prepared to go very far afield and certainly not in the rain. Worried about my timekeeping, she soon presented me with a charming antique watch which no modern strap fitted. "Now Clare will never be late for work," she pronounced optimistically, and I spent a lot of time plaiting straps out of black hat elastic for it before it began to fail. She advised about hair and nails, on no account to be left in their natural state — and commented frankly on dress and appearance in general ("What an *extraordinary* garment!" about something which seemed quite innocuous, "extraordinary", I soon realized, being a synonym for anything unremarkable or drab); and she tried her best to look after our souls too, reminding the Catholics on the staff — of which there were quite a number, if mainly lapsed — about our religious obligations, encouraging us off to noonday mass on holy days at her Monsignor uncle's church in Holborn. She was a wonderful bulwark against officialdom too. Another member of staff famous for being elusive had accumulated an astonishing number of parking tickets without paying the fines, expecting to be off again shortly on his travels. When the exasperated authorities marched in unannounced, demanding to know his whereabouts — he was standing in full view by the fireplace — Jennifer coolly advised them to "Try Venezuela. I think he said he was heading there."

She could be moody, too, of course, and famously resented any interference in the kitchen, which she considered her private domain, in danger of being encroached on by "hordes of beastly advertising people" (only ever about three, and usually charming); but if she believed in *"l'attaque, toujours l'attaque"* her good humour far outweighed any storminess, even if her robust gaiety wasn't to everyone's taste. She teased, cajoled and mocked staff, contributors and guests alike with varying degrees of success. "Oh my goodness, oh my goodness," she used to parody Monty, the gentle, permanently harassed Pakistani accountant who could never pass his accountancy exams but continued to sit them steadfastly anyway, as he shook his head despairingly over the mounting IOUs in the petty-cash box, and perhaps his smile was always a bit perfunctory. She was certainly the only one who dared tease Charles Seaton, the gruff, septuagenarian ex-schoolmaster who had worked at the *Spectator* most of his life and who we were all in awe of. She even discovered that he had been married once — an incredible idea to us — and had lost his wife in a flu epidemic (though perhaps not the 1918 one, as she claimed). "There goes Charlie-Boy!" she used to chant, as he beat a hasty retreat back to his indexing. And there was always chanting, and recitals (one got to know most of *The Importance of Being Earnest* by heart, certainly the part of Lady Bracknell) and singing: opera and musical hall, or "Happy Birthday" to Alec Guinness, Wilfred Thesiger, Enoch Powell and more or less anyone she'd ever come across.

I must have realized even at that time that it wasn't a usual sort of office (which we shared for a while with *The Grower*, a gardening magazine, edited by Mr Bloom, which always seemed to win a lot more awards than we did, and the ghost of a 1950s knitting publication called *Pins and Needles*). I remember a quiet (rare) winter afternoon with Jennifer plucking pheasants at my desk for George Hutchinson, the deputy editor, and on another occasion, flat on the floor, demonstrating with her the game of Moriarty to an unreceptive receptionist. Someone walked in whom we couldn't see, being blindfolded, and walked out again swiftly. I like to think it might have been the same day that Graham Greene had come to lunch, and that perhaps he was returning for his umbrella. The receptionist wouldn't necessarily have known: if it was that day, she had mistaken him for a carpet salesman when he'd arrived and had directed him to the basement. The atmosphere had the added charm of coinciding with the *Spectator*'s renaissance, and for all its eccentricity it was an efficient office for being harmonious, versatile and loyal, and Jennifer epitomized its feeling of casual subversiveness and fun.

Our birthdays were within a week of each other's and we were both Aries ("Aren't we alike!" she would exclaim provocatively). I suppose temperamentally we could hardly have been more different, but we did share many things in common and weren't exactly unalike. And because cooking was so much part of her life she made me take an interest in it, and I learnt a lot more from her. She used to say that her earliest memories of good food were at her convent, which must have made it unique, from which she was soon expelled for being a "disruptive influence" (disruptive mainly of the nuns), the start of a distinguished career of being sacked. Her first present to me was a copy of *French Provincial Cooking*, Elizabeth David being her mentor, followed over the years by a splendid *batterie de cuisine*, though I can't claim to have been a worthy pupil. For the most part entertaining Jennifer was like the old joke about the 1960s — if you could remember it you hadn't been there

93

— though she did always refer to one unfortunate pudding I'd been rather proud of producing: "What is the extraordinary thing you gave us once, dear? Clafoutis? *Clafoutis*!", rolling it round with a pained expression, as if the very word still left a bad taste, and she was right. There can't be many worse inventions than cherries in cold batter, and she wanted to make sure I wouldn't repeat it. But on the whole she had a robust attitude to failure. When a large piece of gammon collapsed in shreds, she rallied the party with, "Never mind, we'll call it 'pulled ham' like the Americans do. I'm sure it will be delicious."

The last time I entertained her I lost my nerve and bought everything in. Then it was, "Very clever, dear, to have produced an entire meal without cooking anything" — a wonderfully double-edged remark. I ate her own food only rarely, and it was always superb, even if some of her receipts were famously haphazard, with essential ingredients missing, and timing depending on how fast you said the Our Father and three Hail Marys, or whether you could remember the Hail Holy Queen at all. It always seemed to be vicars' wives who had the most difficulty with the timing.

Her driving could also be haphazard, though she never had a serious accident, which she attributed to the medal of St Christopher on her handlebars. But we did come close to one once, on a wet evening in the Marylebone Road, when we braked suddenly at traffic lights and disappeared under the wheels of a juggernaut; luckily it was a huge intercontinental model with plenty of room to scramble out before the lights changed. She dusted us both down matter-of-factly, we continued on our way and she treated it with characteristic hilarity, often referring to "the time I nearly killed Clare". But I was anyway always more worried that she was going to kill herself. "Here I go, drunk in charge of a Honda," were invariably her parting, not especially reassuring words after lunch. "Time to go home, time to go home," in a gentle lilt, and then in a muttered aside, *"Time for a whisky!"* Perhaps she did drive best when she was over the limit, as she always claimed. In any case, it was pointless to argue, as she preferred to sleep in her own bed, and I only ever persuaded her to stay once (she was up the next day at 6 a.m., tuned to the Third Programme at full volume, with no sign of a hangover). She delighted in a bureaucratic anomaly which licensed her to drive a Heavy Goods Vehicle and a motorbike, though not a car. Hearing that my sister and her husband had moved to a farm in Wiltshire, she unusually volunteered a trip to the country. "Tell them to ask me to stay. I'll drive the tractor. I'm allowed to."

After our spill in the Marylebone Road she didn't take me out again, though she did take my son, Edward, for short trips (a photograph of them together shows Jennifer turning to check on him, while he looks apprehensive but excited, in her spare crash helmet, aged about four). Like all children he didn't know what to make of her. Not only was she brisk and unsentimental, but she could mimic any child making a fuss and drown them out without effort. Most children, having caught their breath, would scream the louder for being upstaged by this unusual adult behaviour, which led to extraordinary caterwauling on both parts until Jennifer got bored. It wasn't so much that children should be seen and not heard, but that they shouldn't be heard above her. But beneath a show of indifference, almost a wariness of children, she was always generous with presents and quick to help in any predicament. Discovering that Edward had been cast as Zeus in his school play and needed a crown, she immediately came up with one: a magnificent creation of red and silver flames of foil which she'd once made, and worn as the Queen of Sheba.

Like many people who lend themselves to anecdote, Jennifer was a difficult person to know well, and I'm not sure that I did, though she knew me well enough. For all her forthrightness, she had an old-fashioned reserve, and a mistrust of confidences — and confessions of any kind. She scarcely ever reminisced, and seemed untouched by nostalgia, with the possible exception of the Blitz — "Fireworks every night, dear!" — and in fact the whole of the war could more or less be summarized as powdered eggs and camaraderie. But this was in character: she was too vivid a person to live in the past, and one had to be content with what one got of that, and sometimes with quite abstract notions. She attributed her lameness partly to her operation, but partly to her childhood in China. "They do extraordinary things to feet there." One presumed this must have been through some kind of osmosis, but it sounded convincing, and at any rate that was childhood dealt with.

But if she didn't divulge much, she knew things in a way that was uncanny and sometimes disquieting, even guessing that I was pregnant the day after I knew it myself ("I can always tell, dear, I can always tell . . ." rather wearily). She may often have disapproved, but she never preached or admonished — "very unusual" covering most kinds of behaviour — and her advice was always light. Seeing me agonizing over picking a horse for the National, she got exasperated: "Just back the ones with 'Gay' in their names. I always do" — a rule she also applied to lipstick, "Gay Geranium" being a favourite. It was her way, as ever, of saying "Have fun" and of pricking pomposity.

Watching her doodling one day at my desk, I was immediately struck by her talent for drawing, which she was quick to dismiss. "They couldn't think what to do with me after convent, so they sent me to art school." When pressed, she admitted to having had two ambitions, to be an artist or an actress, both of which she fulfilled in her television series, and more than that, stardom. It was wonderful to think of her being mobbed in two continents; even more impressive, perhaps, to think of London taxi drivers crossing lanes to be the ones to hail her after *Two Fat Ladies* ("But I know you, love, you're the thin one!"). If it meant, inevitably, that I saw less of her later in life, it was remarkable how little fame changed her — and fortune not at all, which she seemed bemused by and to regard as a curiosity.

I loved Jennifer simply, the simplest way of all being that I always looked forward to seeing her, whether in the office, or at home, or anywhere else. Hearing her arrive, from a distance, was extraordinarily cheering, and added to the pleasure through anticipation. Before setting off for a party alone, I used often to reassure myself with the thought of her being there; apart from anything else, there was the certainty that she was where the fun would be, at *her* party within the party. She loved her friends and was without jealousy, delighting in introducing them, and delighting in knowing that they liked one another, even if she had a tendency to refer to most of them as "nuts", a term of great affection. I hope I was "nuts" too — but I was glad at least to have been known by her once as "my mucker".

Ruby Red Risotto
SERVES 4

If you're after a receipt for St Valentine's day, try this startling red risotto which I was served by Willie Landels. It is highly original, I should think, amazing to behold and most delicious, though it would make my lovely colleague, Clare Asquith, tremble with horror as she shies from beetroot as I do from spiders.

225g (8 oz) arborio rice
3 medium-size cooked beetroots
250ml (8 fluid oz) milk
900ml (1½ pints) chicken or veal stock
2 tablespoons olive oil
25g (1 oz) butter
1 medium-size onion
150ml (5 fluid oz) red or white wine
salt and freshly ground pepper
fresh Parmesan cheese

✳ Risotto is not a pilaf or anything to do with the dishes requiring that every grain of rice should be separate; it is therefore essential to use the arborio rice which has plump, succulent and absorbent grains. Buy the white grains, never the yellowish ones.

✳ Put the beetroots and the milk in a blender, and whizz until smooth. Have the stock heating in a pouring saucepan. In another saucepan put the olive oil and butter to melt. Peel and chop the onion very finely, add to the oil and cook gently until golden but not brown. Stir in the rice until it is well impregnated with the oil and butter, pour in the wine and let it continue to cook gently until absorbed. Now add 600ml (1 pint) of the stock, cup by cup. Let it cook and absorb, but keep your eye on it, giving the odd stir; pour in the beetroot mixture and season with salt and freshly ground pepper. At the end of the cooking, which will be about 20 minutes, stir continuously to prevent sticking to the bottom of the pan and add the last of the stock if necessary.

✳ The rice should be a creamy consistency like a bowl of porridge but still have a slight bite to it. Add a tablespoon of freshly grated Parmesan cheese, turn off the heat and let it rest for a couple of minutes, when it will be *ben mantecato* as the Italians put it. Serve at once with more Parmesan on the side.

Jennifer at Large

Richard Ingrams
Katharine MacDonogh Glynn
Boyd Harte
Andrew Barrow

Enter Lord Gnome! Richard Ingrams, who delighted a whole generation of lawyers when he edited *Private Eye*, now courts respectability as editor of the *Oldie*. He provided Jennifer with a new showcase for her thoughts on food and saints.

And we hear from three close friends. Katharine MacDonogh knew Jennifer as well as anyone, though whether the latter appreciated Katharine's scholarly interest in royal cats and dogs is open to question. Glynn Boyd Harte, best known for his paintings, some of which formed the basis for books on Venice and the northern coast of France, thought of Jennifer almost as a surrogate mother. Andrew Barrow, novelist and creator of one of the most entertaining books published in the last fifty years, *Gossip*, saw her in a social mode, and calls her "one of the greatest clowns of the twentieth century". The image of Jennifer, with white face and pointed hat, capering in a circus ring and intimidating the children, is curiously seductive.

A Strange and Exotic Mix

Richard Ingrams

Normally on 19 August I would have received a birthday card from Jennifer (she never forgot it), but instead I found myself attending her funeral at Brompton Oratory along with literally hundreds of her friends. It still seems hard to accept that someone so physically and mentally robust, so seemingly indestructible, is dead. Even when I last saw her in hospital, about two weeks before she died, she was the same old Jennifer, surrounded by get-well cards (most of them religious) and with a fridge full of champagne and caviare.

Jennifer contributed her cookery column from the very first issue, defying with typical bravado the disapproval of the *Spectator*'s editor Frank Johnson, who saw the new magazine as a rival and who wished to have exclusive rights on Jennifer. She kept it up until just before her death, never once (as far as I recall) missing an issue. Her copy was often delivered in person, Jennifer arriving in the office in motorcycle gear and a jewelled crash helmet.

It was a strange and exotic mix — just like one of her own recipes (or receipts, as she insisted on referring to them). Her religious observances, her attendance at family celebrations (when she appeared usually in the role of a fairy godmother) were juxtaposed with her receipts, more often than not borrowed — though always with full acknowledgement — from other cookery writers. I was privileged, early on in the column's history, to be given a personal receipt for Sauce Tartare, after I told Jennifer that I was, at the time, living on a diet of fish fingers.

Somewhere along the way, she was rocketed to fame, along with her co-star Clarissa Dickson Wright, with their *Two Fat Ladies* programme. But I don't think her celebrity had the slightest effect on her, any more than the vast quantities of drink she consumed. It was equally true that the Jennifer who appeared on TV was exactly the same person whom you saw in real life. Her success was due to the fact that she was a natural — someone without any artifice or guile.

As readers of her column will have known, Jennifer was an old-fashioned pre-Vatican II Roman Catholic who observed all the high days and holy days with a simple and childlike faith. I often thought she would have made a good Mother Superior, though the nearest she came to it was as matron at Padworth College near Newbury, in which role I first met her, years before we became friends, accompanying Jonathan Routh to a village cricket match with a party of schoolgirls. I did not know, until she died, that Jennifer had had an earlier career on TV as a bit-part actor on Jonathan Routh's famous *Candid Camera* programme — so it is appropriate that, by one of those strange *Oldie* coincidences, Jonathan contributed an article to the same issue on his piles operation. I can imagine Jennifer hooting with laughter over it, as she did over almost everything, including her own fatal illness which sadly robbed her of the retirement she was so keenly looking forward to. May she rest in peace.

Sauce Tartare

Pound three hard egg yolks with a tablespoon of Dijon mustard and a pinch of salt until very smooth, then add about half a pint of olive oil, drop by drop to start with, beating with a wooden spoon until it thickens. Then you can dribble the oil in more generously, thinning the sauce when necessary with a little lemon juice or wine vinegar. Chop finely three tablespoons each of capers, gherkins and fresh green herbs (parsley, chives, tarragon) and mix into the sauce. If truly lazy, use bought mayonnaise, then add the goodies.

Big Jen

Katharine MacDonogh

I first met Big Jen in 1985 at a dinner party. I did not
meet her through my mother although I wish I had
because I might then have had more than the fifteen
years of enjoyment I was allotted. They were
contemporaries at the Convent of the Assumption at
Pegwell Bay in Kent. I asked my mother for some
recollections: joyfully religious, she remembered,
anarchic, lacking application, kind, extrovert, always in
the foreground of any photograph. There she can still be
seen, little different in shape, but *sans* pigtail. It was
plaits then. In that pre-Woodbine era, the cigarettes they
collectively relished were rolled from leaves sought in
the school grounds. In 1939 my mother asked Jen (as she
was known even then) to write a few words in one of
those autograph books so loved by schoolgirls across the
ages:

> You asked me to write in your autograph
> To put something original in
> But I've nothing original in me
> Except original sin

Jen was expelled from school during the war, circa 1943, and sat her school certificate at home. Greatly missed by her peers, she sent one of them a note to reassure them all was well; with the help of gin and rum as *aides-mémoire*, she was merrily preparing herself for her forthcoming examinations.

Some forty years later the thought of reuniting what I could muster of these old convent girls struck me as amusing. Jen was duly invited to dinner with my mother and Ferah Halim, a volatile woman of Egyptian extraction whom I had known in my teens, when I would occasionally babysit her children, and who had once frightened the life out of me as I sat minding my own business in the lavatory by hammering on the door and accusing me of extraordinary perversions. When I finally dared emerge from hiding she greeted me charmingly. It was a case of mistaken identity; she had thought I was her husband. The noise at this dinner was deafening — even Glynn Boyd Harte was reduced to relative silence during this settling of old scores. Not school scores; life's scores. My mother and Ferah, both beauties in their time, had graduated to the more predictable post-convent course in applied nymphomania and emerged in late middle age embittered harpies, swooping and clawing at Jen in their tragic triumphalism. But Jen, joyfully religious Jen, merely peered at them over her spectacles with a look of infinite bemusement and benign wisdom as she listened to the Devil snapping at their heels. Kissing don't last. Cookery do.

Had the absence of husbands and lovers left such a gaping lacuna in Jen's life? Everything indicated the opposite. Beneath her devil-may-care carapace lurked a sensitive creature. The only person towards whom she bore any rancour was her mother, who had once taken her into a shop and asked the assistant's advice on how to dress a baby elephant. As a result she would offer effusive congratulations to anyone whose mother had died. She took a mischievous delight in embarrassing people. She used to enjoy posing outrageous questions while seated on the lavatory with the door open — she was convinced she would die in that position. Her own experiences I would never have dared penetrate although, in the course of the schoolgirls' reunion, she did rather enigmatically reveal that she was a virgin despite having "been poked". Once, in the lift with the two teenage sons of friends, she inquired as to which of them had the notoriously large penis. She took a particular pleasure in subjecting misogynists to enormous bear hugs ("I'm a gender-bender," as she put it). On the subject of children she rather irritatingly claimed to be an expert, a legacy from her au-pairing days. My own daughter, who was slapped hard at the age of three for daring to make a noise in Jen's presence, would beg to differ.

Notwithstanding the tough Catholic line which she took on marriage, Jennifer regarded sex as an immense joke on God's part. Notorious "fag-hag" that she was, claiming without exaggeration that she had had as many faggots at her feet as Joan of Arc, she nonetheless considered homosexuality to be a transitory phase in human sexual development and regretted its legalization. Inviting her to exclusively male dinners was inviting trouble: "too many poofs". Practising homosexuals would be harangued in church as "mortal sinners" and encouraged to leave in a stentorian stage whisper. Similarly, as a very occasional attendant, I would be hauled back to my pew if ever I attempted to approach the communion rail. God, as she regularly reminded us all, will not be mocked.

She got away with this as she got away with everything. It was as though layers of her own thick skin were spontaneously grafted on to the thin pores of her "victims" at the instant of attack and if, as occasionally happened, she caused more hurt than intended, she was invariably forgiven precisely because the offence was inadvertent. There was not a malevolent bone in her body. She never gossiped and was ever loyal to those she considered her friends. Although she found rudeness "very common" she could sail pretty close to the wind herself. One of her pet hates was the Irish and at a dinner of mine where one of the guests was an Irishwoman of marked republican sympathies, she profited from my momentary absence in the kitchen to launch an off-the-hoof theory that the famine was entirely of their own making.

She was far from immune to snobbery, from time to time making a rather dotty claim to be a Countess of the Holy Roman Empire. *Folie de grandeur?* Mercifully transitory. Space permitting, it was nonetheless advisable not to place her at the head of the table, a vantage point from which she was liable to dominate the proceedings even more than was customary. Pomposity, however, she abhorred, in the same way as she did self-congratulation. Anyone sufficiently unguarded as to blow their own trumpet in her presence would find their ears assailed by the full brass of her orchestral wrath. Nor did she have any time for self-pity and no one who witnessed her extraordinary courage in the face of death can accuse her of hypocrisy.

Lacking in application? She would — and frequently did — do anything to avoid work to which she was committed. Until fame fundamentally altered her routine, a normal day in the life of Jen consisted of swimming, drinking, lunching, sleeping, drinking, followed by party or telly. We would sometimes coincide at the pool in Victoria, where she would make a spectacular entrée into the ladies' changing room, booming some song or other to squeals of delight from her "munchlings", the little girls getting dressed to go back to school. It must be said that the sight of her in the pool was fairly amusing, like an enormous sea lion. Keith Day and I used to fantasize about bringing along a great tray of fish and chucking them at her from the gallery.

Stupid she was not, although I suspect she was largely osmotically educated by the wide coterie of intelligent people whose society she frequented. Her great love of music she inherited from the father she adored. It is hard to know when she would have fitted in the time for reading and she hated walking. Plays had to be extremely good to counter the effects of nicotine and whisky withdrawal. It was with some trepidation that

Charles and I took her to see the film *La Vità e Bella* at the cinema a few months before her death. We were worried whether she would stay the course without a drink but she had sensibly brought a hip flask along with her, which she brandished in the foyer. As we gulped down great swigs of vodka the inevitable fans crowded in on her, hopelessly trying to remind her where they had met. She had not a clue. There were too many.

When I first met her Jen was cooking for the *Spectator* and her fame, albeit as yet unleashed on the world at large, was gathering apace. She was invited hither and thither but never reciprocated hospitality. She was perfectly liberal with liquid entertainment in her flat when her uncle was absent but it was never by way of reciprocation any more than were the excursions to restaurants to which she had started to treat us once the penny dropped that she was no longer poor. Overcome with curiosity as to whether she ever ate at home at all, I once ransacked her fridge only to find it devoid of any comestible product whatsoever. There was lipstick, nail varnish, cigars and cigarettes. Jen took her supper but she sang for it, and she had a genius for making her absence from a dinner table more a source of guilt than celebration on the part of the host. When she did come round one could never be sure whom she might have in tow; many a time she would appear with some total stranger picked up in the lift: "Come and meet Mumm and Dadd," she would suggest, and a look of total bafflement would cross the face of someone fully expecting to be confronted by Jen's parents. And she never forgot a birthday. By ringing first thing year in year out to boom her own very individual rendering of "Happy Birthday" down the phone she made any festivities feel wrong without her. The last time I spoke to her was on 9 August 1999, my birthday and the eve of her death. She made a stab at it.

Jen's love of food was fostered at a school where the girls apparently ate extremely well. Food became her *métier* and of course she cooked. The proof was in the columns. I did once taste her famous egg mousse at a lunch given by Tom Hartman and very good it was too. I remember being rather jealous when, a couple of days before we were all to dine with Richard Fowler, she rang to ask if she could make the bread sauce. I remonstrated with her, pointing out it was more than she had ever offered to do for me. "I have no intention of making bread sauce," she announced. "I simply wanted him to get grouse." He did. She taught Charles to time a poached egg to perfection by following the recipe which proved infallible by all practising Catholics: 1 Paternoster + 2 Hail Marys. She could certainly be very critical of everybody else's cooking. I got off rather lightly on the whole, her main criticism being my unfortunate "French habit", as she put it, of never heating the plates. Ian Scott got very short shrift when he accidentally added sugar instead of salt to a salmon mousse. "Absolutely filthy!" she shrieked across the table where the other dinner guests were exhibiting noble British reticence and politely pretending not to have noticed. She had no time for food faddists, particularly vegetarians, and was driven to distraction by the beef-on-the-bone legislation. Bones were a great favourite, to be clasped in those dripping red talons and gnawed with great gusto, sleeves rolled up to the elbow. Christmas represented the high point of the year. She visited several households in the course of the day, picking the carcass clean in each and recycling the gifts she had received in the last, irrespective of whether they were Hermès scarves or bars of soap. The whisky and the Woodbines she kept.

Most of the better-known Jenniferisms involve her culinary exploits. Other than attending the glamorous parties laid on by her beloved Patricia Llewellyn after the filming of each *Two Fat Ladies* series, my only professional association with her occurred when she was asked by the cook Aldo Zilli to appear with five friends at a lunch of his own preparation which was to be filmed as a programme in a television series he was putting together. Summoned to pre-shoot drinks at Jen's flat, Charles and I were presented with a jeroboam of champagne and dosed with generous libations: "You must drink the lot, I hate waste."

Tom Hartman arrived shortly after, announcing menacingly that he had decided to take a day off the good behaviour régime he was then following and gulped down a couple of stiff gins in fairly rapid succession. Eventually, and already somewhat the worse for wear, we clambered aboard the enormous "Jenmobile" which had been sent to collect us and whisked off to Brooklands race track. It transpired that the previous film had involved a party of Essex girls, and the crew, clearly still recovering, were deceived by our superficially respectable appearances into believing they would have a relatively easy run. Jen had warned us that most of filming involved hours of hanging around but we were novices. It was not long before the crew bore a collective expression suggesting that Essex might not be such a bad place after all. By the time we sat down for the famous lunch it was well past six o'clock and we were enjoying ourselves enormously. It was certainly an authentic lunch with Jen. Tom had taught us how to attach spoons to our noses by some curious process of repeated friction and thus we sat with Jen valiantly interjecting the occasional matronly but unconvincing "that will be enough of that" while Tom delivered a hilarious exposé on the effects of Viagra tablets. The shoot was a fiasco; nothing could be salvaged from the wreckage bar the predictable sequence of Jen on her bike.

Long before Jen roared to success in *Two Fat Ladies* the loud woman on her bike was a familiar figure in her neighbourhood, as well as further afield. The first time she gave me a lift was after lunch in Fitzrovia with the Boyd Hartes about ten years ago. We meandered our way back to Victoria through a labyrinth of one-way streets, each approached from the wrong direction. As we sped past a police station my heart sank in anticipation of our imminent arrest but the constable on the steps simply waved and greeted Jen affectionately by name. She had every reason to be well acquainted with "the boys in blue". Her celebrated description of herself as "a spinster of the parish of Westminster" harked back to the time she was stopped after jumping a set of red traffic lights and asked to provide some identification.

She once left a party so tight that she rode straight under an articulated lorry along the Embankment and, had it not been for the uncanny darkness, she reckoned she would never have noticed. My daughter, Hortense, so enjoyed her first spin at the age of five that memories of the slap were soon effaced.

The bike's primary purpose was of course functional. The deceptively small basket actually concealed an Aladdin's cave of recycled gifts, bottles, cigarettes and dishes to be served up at one of her lunches. When she fell to the ground outside the Savoy, clutching her helmet and shrieking, "My brains! My brains!" she was in fact referring to the *cervelles de veau* which had been destined for some function later in the day and now lay splayed across the main entrance to the hotel.

The most touching gift I ever received from Jen was the "Born Wild" helmet which later sat in stately glory on a velvet cushion at the Brompton Oratory during her funeral. I am glad to be able to say that it was not buried with her. Jen had been complaining that she felt unwell since the beginning of the year but it was only in early July, when she refused to come round for a drink, that it dawned on us she might be seriously ill. We lived a stone's throw away. Patricia Llewellyn rushed her off for tests which confirmed all our worst fears. Together we took her to the Chelsea and Westminster Hospital and during the hiatus before a bed was allocated we all went and sat on the pavement outside the bar across the road, where we drank and smoked. A slim and elegant blonde approached and told Jen how much she enjoyed watching her on the television. "Have we met before?"

inquired poor, dizzy Jen, whose head was swimming. "No, but I'm Clarissa's sister," the stranger replied before disappearing along Hollywood Road. A curious little postscript to the series.

As so often in these circumstances, Jen was the only person to have no inkling what was wrong with her and she had heart-rending moments of optimism. We thought it best to be with her when the death sentence was delivered but the "counsellor" arrived early and Patricia had been delayed. I was faced with what I had most dreaded: I found myself alone. He came with an assistant. He had no need. Jen remained totally calm. She told him she came from a family that knew how to die. He asked if there was anything she would like. A moment's reflection. "Yes," she replied, "I would rather like a cigarette", and we laughed. We *laughed*. The last few years of Jen's life had been leaves from a fairytale. She had always believed "God takes you when he wants you" and had fully expected to get her summons some time sooner. The girl who had written "there's nothing original in me" at the age of ten ended up giving her personality to the world in the space of that God-given encore and the world embraced it. The stage shrunk in those last few weeks but she performed to the end before an audience of devoted friends. The fat lady has left a crater in all our lives but I bet they are laughing in Paradise.

Gigot of Monkfish
SERVES 4-6

Visitors to Reggio nell'Emilia in Italy will be surprised to discover that the city's most famous saint, Bishop Prosper, is commemorated not by the great cathedral but by the little church of San Prospero, tucked away behind it in the market square. St Prosper, who died on 25 June in the year 466, built the church outside the walls of Reggio and directed that he should be buried there. But the people of Reggio made him their patron saint and in the year 703 his remains were moved to their present resting-place inside the city walls. He may well be the patron of prosperity, if you need it, but in fact he gave away all his possessions to the poor. A very nice and gentle saint. Twenty-ninth June is the feast of Peter and Paul and I think a fine fish dish is appropriate. I was once given a great deal of cream by my neighbour, Caroline Spencer, and thought this up to use some of it. You can get jars of mushrooms in large supermarkets.

tailpiece of monkfish, 0.5-1.5kg (1-3 lb)
2 plump cloves garlic, cut into fine slivers
Maldon salt and freshly ground black pepper
olive oil
120ml (4 fluid oz) dry vermouth or Chambéry, warmed
275g (10 oz) preserved wild mushrooms in oil
175ml (6 fluid oz) thick cream
1 tbsp chopped parsley
1 tbsp chopped tarragon
lemon juice

✻ Preheat the oven to 220°C/425°F/Gas 7.

✻ Ask the fishmonger to remove the membrane from the fish or do it yourself. Place the fish in a suitable oven-proof dish. Insert the slivers of garlic with a sharp knife. Season well with Maldon salt and freshly ground pepper and anoint with olive oil. Cover and place in the preheated oven for 15 minutes, then turn the heat down to 180°C/350°F/Gas 4. Add the warmed vermouth or Chambéry, and cook for a further 30 minutes, basting occasionally.

✻ When the fish is just about done, add the mushrooms, cream, parsley and tarragon, adjust the seasoning and add a little lemon juice to taste. Stir everything together, basting the fish, and return to a hot oven, 220°C/425°F/Gas 7, for 5 minutes.

✻ Serve in the cooking dish with plain new potatoes, and I added samphire, but hot cucumber would be good.

Clearing up after Me Mother

Glynn Boyd Harte

The very first time I met Jennifer Paterson we were thrown out of the Chelsea Arts Club for making too much noise. I was an art student, and my friend Katharine MacDonogh had invited me to meet her mother and a couple of her mother's school chums.

Katharine's mother I had already met, rather a raddled Viennese jewellery designer with touches of glamour, and there in the club she was with some sort of Egyptian princess on one side and in the middle Jennifer, foursquare and Buddha-like, black lacquer hair smoothed into a chignon, crimson Cupid lips and a sort of spherical tight-fitting fuchsia-coloured cotton smock. Jennifer eyed me balefully through enormous horn-rimmed spectacles. *"Who's this?"* she boomed imperially, and then, softening a little, said, "We were having a little drink, honey" as she poured me an enormous vodka. Shades of *Vile Bodies* made me rather nervous. All three had been to the same convent, and I think all three had been expelled, but for different reasons and at different times.

Quite soon all three former little maids from school were contentedly shouting at the top of their voices, the Egyptian often lapsing into an unknown tongue, interspersed with wild ululations, while the Viennese now and again burst into sobs and Jennifer simply boomed. Katharine, calmly drinking her drink, was obviously used to her mother's friends and I was merely mesmerized.

When the Egyptian's ululations began to sound like the turbines on the Aswan Dam, Jennifer, determined not to be upstaged, abruptly stood up and began to sing. Without any prompting and with a voice twice as deep and fifty times louder than Bessie Smith, she launched into: "What is this thing called love? *Honey*!"

She then roared with laughter: I was enchanted: we were asked to leave.

On the cold dark quiet pavement outside Jennifer started getting on her moped. "Can I call you mother?" I asked. Jennifer froze in the mid-action of putting on her helmet, crimson lips in full moue.

"I am a spinster of this parish," she said, coyly doing up her helmet. On her helmet it said "BORN WILD" in bold lettering.

"I have forgiven you, Mother."

She gave a snort, then, looking over her shoulder, shouted back, *"He always was a stupid child"* as she roared off into the night.

Several years later John Murray — that formerly great publishing house — was going to publish her first collection of recipes (or receipts as Jennifer tiresomely always called them) she had written for the *Spectator* and they asked me to illustrate it and provide a front cover.

I can't remember now quite how this came about, but it could hardly be on me mother's recommendation. She would always loudly say, *"He can't draw."*

Jennifer had by now performed her fabulous career move. In the famous episode of flinging everything out of the *Spectator*'s office window she had instantly progressed from cook to character and not only a character but a character with a column. At the time, I think none of us thought it would end up so global. Fans would drool with delight to read about the more obscure saints of the Roman Catholic religion, with a recipe for walnut cake thrown in at the end, usually contributed by a dear friend and often printed without several of the vital ingredients so that, along with the famous "Jeffrey Bernard is unwell", we would be delighted to read the following week that "Miss Paterson inadvertently omitted the walnuts from her walnut cake recipe and suggests you use four ounces".

Jennifer, notoriously, had been cooking weekly lunches for the *Spectator*, and immediately I was commissioned for the cover of the book I had a vision of her on her moped crossing London on her way there, the modest little moped being transformed into a lavish cornucopia of sausages, lobsters, braces of partridges, a Methuselah of champagne and other sumptuous things. It was an idea later taken up, I notice, by the television company.

Jennifer was enthusiastic about the idea and came round several times for lunch and afterwards

(afterwards, ha!) to pose for me. We were living then in Percy Street, a house large enough to contain her, and she would arrive with her usual booming barrage, *"He's got no taste. He can't cook"*, bearing a bottle of vodka, which she knew we didn't usually drink at lunchtime. After lunch, and before it got too dark, she would pose for me on her moped outside on the street, swinging sausages, swinging vodka and bellowing Bessie Smith. I have often wondered what the office workers all could have made of this.

When I had practically finished, with only a final sitting to go, I received a letter from the publishers saying that they wanted to see a rough, and that on *no account* should a picture of Miss Paterson appear on the book since it would be guaranteed to put the public off. The next day Jennifer arrived to finish the portrait: I had left the letter, open, on the sofa table. Jennifer read it and simply snorted, "I know more people than they do . . ."

I am afraid the publisher was presented with a *fait accompli*, and so the fat lady on a bike was born. In the finished book, some quirk of printing did rather emphasize the shadow under her nose.

When Jennifer saw the printed version she simply growled, "You've made me look just like Adolf Hitler, honey."

One of the sweetest and most beguiling things Jennifer would do was never forget your birthday. I think she did this to all her friends, and not only mine but also my wife's and children's.

Whether we were here or in France, early in the morning the telephone would ring, and there would be

Bessie gravelling, "Happy birthday to you, honey" and then roaring with laughter. It was the same great roar of laughter that she shared with John Betjeman, and these two wonderful people (I would have liked to adopt Betjeman as my father but didn't quite dare) shared a great zest for life, all its eccentricities and the whole comedy of living.

Almost the last time I saw Jennifer was at my fiftieth birthday party, a "red and black" affair at the Art Workers' Guild in Queen's Square. By this time Jennifer was a mega global celebrity and it rather showed. Her stately entrance, swathed in an enormous Day-Glo red feather boa, was met with applause, but another friend interrupted the procession by stopping her, introduced herself, then said they had a friend in common. "*Who?*" boomed Jennifer. My friend mentioned a name. "Never heard of her," snapped Jennifer as she flicked her boa about her and recommenced her progress. Of course I knew she would not drink red wine and had brought her own little cache of Black Label whisky. Soon she was glugging away, sitting, cigarette in hand, happily, surrounded by cardinals and a smattering of devils. She was in her element.

The next day I had to go in and clear up. I found fifty-five unsuspected summer puddings under a table. It was not difficult to find where my mother had been sitting. On the floor surrounding her seat lay three or four discarded whisky bottles embedded in a pile of cigarette ash and broken glass, but what was worse was Jennifer had enacted a brilliant revenge for having the cabaret inflicted on her: her boa began to moult. Just a few feathers around the throne to start with, but then a distinct trail led to the ladies' loo upstairs. Every feather had to be carefully picked up, all evidence of the presence of a Day-Glo feather boa at the Art Workers' Guild just had to be eradicated. I have never entered the ladies' loo before, and did so with trepidation. I gasped with horror. What had previously been the fall of a few feathers had now turned into a frenzy. There were feathers in the basins, all over the mirrors, on the ceiling and up to your ankles on the floor. What had happened? Had a fox got at her? And then I burst into laughter: after all, what is the point of a child if it's not to clear up after its mother?

The very last time I saw Jennifer was at a cocktail party high up in those grim dark streaky-bacon flats in that beloved area of hers surrounding Westminster Cathedral. Fittingly, it was a party given by Katharine MacDonogh, who had first introduced us all those years ago. My mother seemed very changed and even, unbelievably, vulnerable. It was only a few days before she finally entered hospital, but she made an effort and an entrance. She held up a withered arm. "Look what I got in Scotland," she said, and added, "or was it in Jamaica?"

I asked her how she was. The moue lips replied, "I've got Outsiders' Disease."

"But, Mother, we've all got Outsiders' Disease here — we were born with it."

"I don't mean Outsiders', I mean Outpatients' Disease. I've got Outpatients' Disease." Then, slowly turning to the person next to her, she said, "He always was a stupid child."

125

Sudden Death
SERVES 4

My friend Ian Scott called one day asking for the receipt of the killer chocolate pudding from Patricius Senhouse, my old china from Cumberland. Here it is.

225g (8 oz) digestive biscuits
225g (8 oz) Menier chocolate or the like
225g (8 oz) unsalted butter
50g (2 oz) caster sugar
2 eggs
50g (2 oz) chopped walnuts
50g (2 oz) chopped glacé cherries
85ml (3 fluid oz) rum, brandy or whisky

✳ Grease and line a 450g (1 lb) tin or container. No cooking is required, so it can be anything that takes your fancy.

✳ Crush the biscuits roughly in a plastic bag.

✳ Melt the chocolate in a bowl set over hot water. Cream the butter and sugar, then gradually beat in the eggs until thick and frothy. Fold in the chocolate, biscuits, nuts, cherries and liquor. Pour into the tin and chill overnight. (It can also be frozen.) Turn out and decorate with more cherries and walnuts. Serve with whipped cream. Force yourself.

The Importance of Not Being Earnest

Andrew Barrow

I am pretty certain I first met Jennifer on the uncarpeted stone staircase at Viva King's house in Thurloe Square. Viva had given a party here every Sunday evening since the middle of the Second World War. "What would we do without Viva!" people sighed with admiration as yet another invitation arrived to that exotic household. For me, a late and unlikely recruit to that louche new world, those evenings were eye-opening exposures to a grand, artistic side of London I hadn't known existed and was half-frightened to know too much about. Many of Viva's friends were incredibly distinguished and incredibly odd.

Jennifer fitted beautifully into this milieu: noisy and naughty, she struck old-fashioned poses that gave extra *oomph* to the party. On our first encounter, I nervously asked her what her name was and received the dismissive declamation, "I'm Mrs Patrick Campbell!" I was sufficiently ignorant about almost everything at this time — I think it was about 1969 — that this illustrious name meant nothing to me.

Jennifer Paterson's personality had been fully formed long before the Swinging Sixties. Her name had the schoolgirlish bounce of the 1940s and there were echoes about her of more distant decades. Her speech was littered with phrases like "my good man" and "my dear fellow". Her favourite hotel was the dear old Goring and her family friends had included Radclyffe Hall, who had given the infant Jennifer "a sweet little carpet-sweeper". Throughout her life, she adhered to "Society" in its more outmoded sense, with or without Roman Catholic trimmings and partly populated by rather volatile bachelor-types. Her rôle as a fag hag had never bothered her — "It's in the family, dear. My mother had every queen in Venice on her doorstep" — though she later grumbled that homosexuality was not quite what it was. "The glamour went out of it when they made it legal." Shortly after I met her, Jennifer's ringing tones were well employed as Lady Bracknell in a stylishly amateur production of *The Importance of Being Earnest*. A real-life vicar played Chasuble and Viva King was Prism.

Did Jennifer visit me in the bachelor basement I occupied in Oakley Street during the 1970s? I only remember her shouting, "Good morning, Andrew!" as she sailed past on her motorbike without stopping and without any idea whether I was there or not. Later she suggested that I should buy myself a set of copper saucepans so that some girl would then marry me for my saucepans. I also remember an encounter in a King's Road supermarket, which Jennifer immediately turned into an uproarious social event better than most parties.

Until the last year or two of her life, Jennifer was seriously impoverished and living out of a suitcase, but she seemed to have a lot of fun on no money and always enjoyed combative relationships with the rich and titled. "Are you Lord Smiley's boy?" she asked the journalist Xan Smiley. "Yes," he replied, to keep the ball rolling, though no such lord exists. "Little Lord Moore!" she loudly exclaimed when the photographer Derry Moore slipped quietly into the room. Meeting the young cross-bench peer Valerian Freyberg, she immediately threatened to add him to her rota of "little lordlings". One of her richer friends was the unhappy oil heiress Olga Deterding. In the 1970s Jennifer often acted as master of ceremonies at various parties in Olga's triplex apartment overlooking Green Park, pushing around her fellow guests at whim and wringing a smile from her sad friend when she facetiously suggested that they should live together and become the most famous lesbian couple in London. When Olga Deterding choked to death on New Year's Eve, Jennifer was one of the very few people permitted to attend the funeral.

At this time Jennifer was briefly perching above her station in an Eaton Square flat belonging to Violet, Duchess of Westminster. Here a Viva King-ish atmosphere created by fine French furniture was strengthened by a large equestrian portrait of the duchess in earlier times. I remember Jennifer opening the fridge to reveal the heavy weighting devices she was using to make perfect cucumber sandwiches. I also remember lunching here with Jennifer's two unmarried uncles, Francis and Anthony. When the cook was out of the room, they tut-tutted that their niece always undercooked game birds. When I naughtily repeated this observation, Jennifer was mortally offended. For a split second.

Looking back, I cannot claim to have got very close to Jennifer and we certainly had none of those tiresome fallings-out which characterized some of her more intimate friendships. Yet seeing her motorbike outside a party immediately raised my spirits and her presence was always reassuring. I suppose we were primarily drinking companions and a relationship developed in the vapours of vodka is not necessarily a deep one. Anyway, she would have thought it "common" to ask questions and exchange intimacies about one's inner life. I enjoyed her company best in crowded rooms and I was intrigued by her drinking routines: vodka on the rocks in the morning, whisky at night and white wine in any circumstances. I was also impressed to learn that when travelling by British Rail she brought her own drinks, ice and napkins and, thus equipped, had been in the position to offer a drink to an eminent fellow-traveller, Cardinal Hume. The nonplussed British Rail steward was inspired to ask, "Are you two together?"

In modern times Jennifer often came to lunch or dinner in my Kensington studio. She never had a flat of her own and said she envied my arrangements in Eldon Road. The shrieks that accompanied her arrival were exciting to hear but my cooking would often disappoint. "You normally buy in, don't you?" she said, but when I attempted to cook something it was not always a success. "I don't know what you've done with these steaks," she protested as I hung my head in shame. Her visits were always followed by carefully phrased thank-you notes. "Lunch was delicious after the mistake meat," she wrote on one occasion and on another, "Your cheeses were well-chosen — what a treat — & the other things, except the messed-up chicken, were delicious." On her very last visit I urged her to stay the night on my sofa, and this she did, writing afterwards that she had woken at 5.30a.m. thinking she was in a conservatory, kept warm all night by an electric blanket, and had driven off to her own bed.

Other outings with Jennifer stay in my mind. One Sunday morning I attended Mass with her at Brompton Oratory, at which the priest's proclamation "Any form of sex outside of marriage is a mortal sin" drew a loud "Hear, hear" from my companion. Another Sunday lunchtime I drove Jennifer from Ashley Gardens to the McEwens's house in Camden Town. She had already prepared her vodka on the rocks in one of those cheap mustard jars with a detachable lid and she sipped from this as she expertly directed me to St Augustine's Road. One night, at a dinner at the Travellers' Club given by her "beloved" A. N. Wilson, she created a commotion that she had been served crab rather than lobster mousse but the head waiter took this nit-picking in good heart. Another night I took Jennifer to an old musical comedy and from the front row of the stalls she muttered, "Poof!" as the leading male stepped on stage.

Jennifer was a famous London figure long before she became "our national treasure", and her very special character must have been well established from those childhood days when her greatest treat, she says, was to be "brought up a little snipe to crunch". Others will write about her innate goodness, the role of Roman Catholicism in her life, her astounding contentment on her deathbed — or perhaps speculate about the traces of bitter boredom that may have lain behind all that laughter. Many thought of her as a frustrated actress, who might conceivably have managed a great Shakespearian role. As far as I am concerned, she was an exuberantly wayward *grand'mère terrible*, who could be as mischievous as a small child or as scowlingly sombre as a Venetian cardinal. She was also one of the greatest clowns of the twentieth century, who gave an almost non-stop performance from the moment we first met.

Patrick's Bread and Butter Pudding
SERVES 4

My friend and fellow cook Patrick Williams is also a fine flautist, but in 1987 he was involved in a collision with a juggernaut whilst riding his bicycle and lost all his front teeth, not good for flautists. However, after five years of painful dental surgery the teeth are back and he can play the flute once more. He has his own strong views about cooking which he does superbly, and this is his family's method of making proper bread and butter pudding. I shall relate it to you as told to me. The essential ingredients are stale baguettes and Irish whiskey.

unsalted butter, softened
stale baguettes
raisins or currants
sugar
3 eggs
600ml (1 pint) milk
Irish whiskey

✱ Butter a soufflé dish lavishly with softened unsalted butter. Cut the stale baguettes into rather thin slices, crusts and all, some to line the dish, the others to make up the bulk. Butter each slice, again lavishly. Press the buttered side to the wall of the dish, then fill up the well with the rest of the slices buttered side down, sprinkling raisins or currants in between the layers; the last layer should be butter-side up and sprinkled with sugar.

✱ For the "custard", the ratio is three whole eggs to one pint of milk. Blend the eggs and milk (half cream if you prefer), add a little sugar to taste and a very generous slug of Irish whiskey. Pour all this over the bread. Place in another bowl to catch overflow, then press down. Cover with a bit of foil and place weights on top. Leave for at least six hours overnight. Pour the overflow back into the pudding and place in a preheated oven at 230°C/450°F/Gas 8, for 30-40minutes, after which it will rise above itself like a lovely soufflé.

Fame and Fortune?

Christopher Sinclair-Stevenson
Patricia Llewellyn
Freddie Foster
Clarissa Dickson Wright
A. N. Wilson

After a reflection on the book which Jennifer might have written, we enter the period when *Two Fat Ladies* divided the nation. Some deplored the crimson fingernails, the approach to cooking so unlike Delia Smith's, the ad-libbing and the stories, the overall non-political correctness. Others gloried in the television series, devised brilliantly by Patricia Llewellyn, for precisely the same reasons. Divided or not, the nation watched, avidly. And so did the Australians and the Americans. Here we have the inside track from behind the camera. We also have the view from the market, seen through the eyes of Freddie Foster, who sold Jennifer truffles and smoked garlic at Pimlico Market.

And we have Jennifer's co-star, the other Fat Lady, the inimitable Clarissa Dickson Wright.

Finally there is A. N. Wilson's valediction. Another former literary editor of the *Spectator*, biographer, historian and novelist, he spoke it eloquently and movingly at the glorious Memorial Mass (Mozart, Verdi and of course Latin) for Jennifer at the London Oratory. It is the perfect way to take leave of someone Andrew called "the spouting well of joy".

The Book That Got Away

Christopher Sinclair-Stevenson

There was something exaggerated, almost excessive, about Jennifer. I don't mean just her girth, or her booming voice. I suppose I am thinking of her atmosphere. It is a well-known obituarist's cliché to say that someone "was larger than life". Usually this is a polite way of saying that so-and-so was rampantly oversexed, given to falling down dead-drunk at parties, and displayed various rather depressing signs of extreme eccentricity (aka tiresomeness).

Jennifer could, of course, be very tiresome. She drank not always modestly, she had certain snobberies which could be construed, perhaps misconstrued, as downright rudeness or as social behaviour overlaid with rather too much political incorrectness. Not much fun for those of whom she disapproved, but very jolly for those who assumed they were on the side of her particular angels.

Which brings us to more spiritual rather than spirituous matters. Her Catholic faith was undoubted, sincere, though a trifle sentimental. She enjoyed the full trappings of Church ritual, the so-called smells and bells, everything done in the good old way, in Latin, with good music and a big choir. She took enormous pleasure in tying her receipts (never, as we know, recipes, which has always struck me as a perfectly sound word) to the saint of the day or the week. Being a cynic, I often reflected that this was one of the simplest ways of finding copy. St Sharon (not a name Jennifer would have recognized) was martyred in Anglo-Saxon Essex by being turned into a stew. Splendid. We'll base our piece on a casserole or ragout, but with saintly overtones.

I suppose I was always aware of Jennifer, years before I met her. She was a legend among the chattering classes long before she began zooming up and down the British Isles, terrifying the natives, being gracious to farmers or oyster-gatherers or the local WI. Her niece worked for me in my publicity department and would occasionally mention her mad aunt. It seemed to me that she paled rather at the thought of this formidable relation. She was a gentle girl, and probably did not care to be lectured on her lack of ebullience, or whatever.

Then came the *Spectator* days. As all good publishers should, I was fortunate enough to know a succession of Literary Editors at that admirably self-confident organ. Some of them left under clouds of their own making, some trailing clouds of glory; they were certainly never dull. Nor was the resident cook: Jennifer Paterson. One cannot pretend that her dishes were haute cuisine, but they went perfectly with the bibulous atmosphere. I felt rather honoured to be there, not least because the guest list was odd but amusing, not least because there was always the anticipation of Jennifer committing one of her excesses. The stories of distinguished politicians having their hair ruffled by her rarely over-clean fingers, or famous visiting statesmen being told to eat up, or entire services of china being chucked through the window: these were, to use another obituarist's cliché, legendary.

But it was her method of transport which impressed so many. It wasn't just the motorbike, or the speed at which she rode it. Far more striking was her headgear. I daresay that I imagined this but I do recall vividly her evening style of helmet. There seemed to be plumes and sequins and stars and flashing lights, though no flowing scarves which might have entangled her in the side mirror of some juggernaut. Jennifer was not exactly one's idea of Isadora Duncan. Queen Elizabeth reviewing her troops at Deptford, Boadicea going to war with her scything wheels, one of the Valkyries hooting her way to Valhalla, even Margaret Thatcher declaiming "Enjoy" rather than "Rejoice". That was more the thing.

It was the last period of her life when I got to know Jennifer. Soon after I had ceased to be a publisher and became an agent, I received a telephone call. The voice was instantly recognizable, even though I hadn't clapped ears on her for some time. "I hear you've become an agent, dear. Charles Moore and Andrew Wilson say I should come to you." I didn't hesitate for a second (it was better not to hesitate with Jennifer). So I instantly became her agent. My duties were hardly onerous. She was at the peak of her fame. Publishers were eager to get her to write introductions to cookery books, or to gather together her pieces from the *Spectator* or the *Oldie*.

I began to feel I wasn't doing enough. One of her publishers had the ingenious idea of asking her to write a novel. I raised the subject with Jennifer. "What a ridiculous idea, dear. I couldn't do it, I've got no imagination. Far better to ask Clarissa. She's got bags of imagination." But I never did ask the other Fat Lady. Instead I thought I would work out the plot myself, perhaps even write it with Jennifer, on the principle that she would gradually get drawn into the whole faintly absurd enterprise. Here is what Jennifer might have written, if she had followed my proposal. It would have been fun — and of course she had plenty of imagination. A lost opportunity, if ever there was one.

Too Many Cooks
by Jennifer Paterson

I think this should be a thoroughly old-fashioned detective story, rather in the Christie mould, but with added spice. The setting could be one of those mildly sinister Scottish baronial houses in Aberdeenshire, utterly fake of course, but with plenty of towers, crenellations, staircases, galleries — and extensive kitchens well below stairs. Formerly the home of an Edinburgh merchant who made good in the middle of the nineteenth century and wished to demonstrate to the world that he had risen in society, it was decked out with all the atmospheric fripperies of Scottish Baronial, with a few more modern appurtenances like bathrooms to give a gloss to the starkness of the grouse moor and the salmon river. The merchant's son wasted his inheritance and the family fortunes had to be rescued by the grandson, who sensibly married an American heiress. But even her money could not last for ever, and what with two World Wars and a great many death duties, by the 1950s the only solution was to sell.

A few new owners did very little to the structure, except to put in central heating. In 1975 it became a (very classy) country hotel with a formidable reputation for its cuisine. So celebrated did it become that in the food-conscious 1990s it was annually given over for one week a year to a gathering of famous chefs from America, France, the eastern Mediterranean, the Far East, and the United Kingdom and Ireland.

This is the background. As the book opens, the contestants gather, for in essence they are taking part in a kind of foodie gladiatorial contest, showing off their latest creations, duelling with lemon grass, exotic fish and even the local produce: salmon, game, wild mushrooms. Every night they display their best efforts, and three food critics will adjudge at the end of the week. The opportunities for backbiting and indeed backstabbing are only too obvious.

In late autumn the Highlands of Scotland are frequently cut off by snow or torrential rain. Telephone wires come down. The winds whistle round the turrets and parapets. Vertiginous steps become iced over and dangerous. And in the kitchens it is so easy to serve up a less than fresh oyster, or a woodcock with an unusual stuffing, or a lethal Japanese fish. A walk beside a salmon river turned into a raging torrent should not be undertaken by the infirm or unwary. And then there is the egotism and furious tempers of some of the chefs. Put together in the same house, say, a former footballer whose rages reduce staff to quivering jellies: an arrogant Deep South cook whose use of chillies is perhaps over-generous; an expert on fish who is not too keen on freshness; a Frenchman who despises anyone who comes from any other country but France; a chef from Japan who knows quite as much about Russian roulette as he does about cooking; a television star who cannot really cook at all and whose dishes are prepared by others simply for his final touch; a saintly woman in whose mouth butter wouldn't melt but whose way with a Sabatier knife is, well, cutting. There are naturally no similarities to real people. Equally naturally, the atmosphere, like one of the participants in this drama, could be cut with a knife.

And as the bodies fall, there are two wonderfully eccentric ladies, cooking and solving.

At Jennifer's funeral the great and the not so good, the people she worked with during the making of the *Two Fat Ladies* and the fans who gloried in so much out-and-out "who the hell cares" attitude emanating from those orange lips and painted fingernails on screen, were marking the passing of a phenomenon. Jennifer was hardly a great cook, she was certainly not a great writer (nor would she have for a moment claimed to be either), but she was a figure. People knew about her, in America and Australia just as in Britain. People came up to her in the street and asked for her autograph, and she was very pleased and very nice to the seeker. Suddenly she was very rich, after years of scraping and skimping, but the change in her fortune seemed to have no effect. She simply did not know how to spend money. Her style of life did not change. She didn't dress differently or eat and drink differently. She enjoyed her celebrity, but knew perfectly well that it wouldn't last. "Flash in the pan, dear," reaching for a culinary metaphor.

But it was a very enlivening flash.

Whisky Galore
SERVES 6-8

The beautiful Veronica Hodges, who is an extremely good egg and runs Life for the Unborn Child, gave me the most disgusting-sounding receipt for a pudding, which in fact turned out rather delicious. It came from a rabbi, which should tell us something.

1 heaped teaspoon cocoa
1 heaped teaspoon instant coffee
1 packet gelatine (11g/0.4 oz)
175ml (6-8 fluid oz) boiling water
1 tin of condensed milk (385g/13½ oz)
1 tin of evaporated milk (400g/14-15 oz)
1 tumbler whisky (300ml/6-8 fluid oz)

✳ You could use brandy or rum for this if you prefer, and I find a good sprinkling of freshly ground coffee over the finished jelly gives a certain oomph and texture to the wobbly whole.

✳ Mix the cocoa, instant coffee and gelatine together then dissolve completely with the boiling water. Combine the two tins of milk, stir in the whisky and the gelatine mixture. Pour into a mould and leave to set in the refrigerator. Turn out when ready and serve with a crunchy sweet biscuit: brandy snaps would be excellent I should think.

Behind the Camera

Patricia Llewellyn

I met Clarissa first. She had a small but unforgettable rôle in a food series I was working on where she argued for the return of the cardoon to the British dining table. These forgotten vegetables are huge edible thistles and something of an acquired taste. I can't pretend our meeting changed my opinion of the cardoon — muddy-tasting celery doesn't do much for me — but I certainly acquired a taste for working with Clarissa and spent many months trying to find ways to put her in front of the camera again. I thought she would be good alongside another presenter and I talked to many but none had the necessary force of character and depth of passion to be her counterpart. It was my friend Basil Comely who, after being introduced to Jennifer at a party, urged me to meet her.

Jennifer shared a flat with her elderly uncle Anthony and their voices on the telephone were virtually indistinguishable to a stranger. Our first few telephone conversations were riddled with confusion on my part, as I was constantly thinking Anthony was Jennifer and Jennifer, Anthony. Jennifer rather enjoyed the confusion because she loved playing tricks. Uncle Anthony is a saintly man who dedicates his life to good works and to the Catholic Church. While Jennifer shared his faith, on occasion she lacked his saintliness and got so fed up with taking his messages that she would shout down the receiver in a furious Irish accent that she was his mistress and that he was too drunk to come to the phone.

At our first meeting I asked Jennifer if she was married. "No, no, dear. I'm a spinster of the parish of Westminster. What about you?" I wasn't married either, but at the age of thirty-one Jennifer declared me far too old. "What you need to do is find yourself a nice poof to take you about. They're often jolly good dancers. And with any luck you might get a good jewel from their mother."

Before the BBC would commission a series of *Two Fat Ladies* they wanted to see a pilot to get some idea of how it might work. It was a memorable shoot. Jennifer was an accomplished motorcyclist, but her experience of steering with a sidecar was limited. After a number of perfect takes we had one final shot to achieve. Jennifer was to drive herself and Clarissa towards the camera, stop and deliver a few lines. As the cameraman and I stood behind the camera, watching our Ladies speeding towards us, our sound recordist, who could hear things we couldn't, began waving his arms frantically. Jennifer had got the brakes and gears mixed up — they were the other way round on her own bike. The motorbike and sidecar mowed down the camera tripod and disappeared into the distance. The distance ended a hundred yards away when they hit a flagpole. It was the beginning but it could so nearly have been the end.

The programme was a surprise success in Britain, confounding those who thought its appeal would stop at the home counties. In fact *Two Fat Ladies* was sold to seventy countries. Between 1996 and 1999 we made twenty-four programmes, produced four cookbooks, went on publicity trips to America and Australia, and Jennifer and Clarissa became unlikely international celebrities. They appeared in commercials and on the top chat shows, and performed on stage at the London Palladium for the Prince of Wales's fiftieth birthday. (The Prince had previously declared *Two Fat Ladies* his favourite television programme.)

Jennifer never took her health seriously and regarded those whose minor ailments sent them rushing to the doctor as wastrels. For her generation the doctor was very much the last resort and the discomforts of illness something to be ignored rather than submitted to. On several occasions she had terrible problems with her feet and yet insisted that we carry on filming. So when halfway through the fourth series she was too ill to get out of bed, it was immediately clear to me that something was very wrong. Even then she tried to refuse the offer of a BBC doctor. The doctor came and she was admitted to the Chelsea and Westminster Hospital. A few days later lung cancer was diagnosed. My life hit a flagpole. I always thought Jennifer would be in my life for ever. In three and a half years rarely a day had passed without a meeting or a phone call.

When the press found out Jennifer was ill, journalists eager for a scoop began to try to get into her hospital room. For security reasons the hospital suggested we change her name on the computer and the ward's noticeboard. "I've always wanted to be a Dame or a Lady," Jennifer told her friend David Queensberry. Between them they came up with the perfect moniker and minutes later it was written up on the noticeboard in green marker pen. And so it was that for the rest of her stay Jennifer was known as Lady Vita Circumference. This, as with so many moments in her stay in hospital, was pure Evelyn Waugh — an impression bolstered by the fridge full of caviare in her room sent by well-wishers after she complained her room was overflowing with flowers and she'd rather have something to eat instead of the "disgusting" hospital food. Jennifer was enormously touched when the Prince of Wales sent her a vat of organic soup and some ice cream from his private kitchens along with a handwritten get-well note. She hugely enjoyed the food but it provided us with a difficult social conundrum. What was the etiquette for dealing with the Tupperware containers it had arrived in? Should she send them back? Could she keep them? If she did, what would be right and proper to put in them?

After only eight days in hospital Jennifer's condition took a rapid nosedive. She developed an infection and her weakened immune system was unable to fight it off. A priest was called and gave her the last rites. It seemed like the end. Then came a resurgence that I suspect was driven by Jennifer's passion for a good anecdote. It seemed that receiving the last rites was too good a story not to live to tell. Jennifer recovered in hours and was soon on the telephone proudly telling everyone, "I've had extra muncheon" — a Jenniferism for extreme unction. It cheered her up enormously. "I'm in a state of grace, dear," she would boast to visitors.

Jennifer found diverse ways to amuse herself in her hospital bed. One of her favourites was to go through my make-up bag, laughing at its range of lotions and potions. She was horrified that anyone should buy make-up from anywhere but Boots — her favourite shop and the only place she ever enjoyed shopping. It was from Boots that she bought her favourite lipstick, a lurid orange called Gay Geranium that somehow looked fabulous on her. Boots also provided her with the catarrh pastilles she would never leave home without. The principal task of these foul-smelling lozenges was to ward off errant policemen who might stop her as she wove along on her moped between drinks parties. Their pungent aroma could hide anything on the breath and guarantee that conversation was kept to an absolute minimum.

Her interest in Boots was as girlie as Jennifer ever got. She had a handful of close women friends but mostly she preferred the company of men. In 1997 *Two Fat Ladies* won a Women In Film And Television award for creative ingenuity. After the prize-giving an earnest young journalist asked Jennifer if she was proud to be sitting among all these successful women. "Certainly not," she replied. "I hate it. I'd much rather be sitting next to a man."

Over the course of her four and a half weeks in hospital, Jennifer's bedroom became a kind of old-fashioned literary salon as friends visited and were encouraged to drink, whatever time of the day or night. Jennifer was usually fastidious about her drinking: vodka before 3p.m. and whisky after 5.30p.m. (with a siesta in between), but hospital mealtimes played havoc with her Mediterranean habits. One morning I rang her at 9.30. Responding to my usual "Still alive then?" (I learned quickly that this was the best way to ask Jennifer how she was), she boomed into the phone, "I've got Beryl Bainbridge and Anna Haycraft [Alice Thomas Ellis] here. They're having a whisky."

In life Jennifer refused to suffer fools gladly, and she saw no reason why illness should change that. One day, when a couple of friends and I were at her bedside, an unwelcome guest was announced. Jennifer shooed us into the bathroom, where we stifled giggles as she feigned near unconsciousness, lying back and moaning loudly. As expected, the visitor left almost immediately. On another occasion I rang her and was shocked to hear her answer the phone in a pathetic little voice, far removed from the Jennifer I knew so well. "Hello," she half whispered. "Hello," I said. "Still alive then?" At this she instantly returned to her normal self, booming down the phone, "Oh it's you, dear. Thank God, I thought it was another bloody do-gooder."

For years Jennifer and I had joked that she'd probably die halfway through making the last *Two Fat Ladies* programme. I'd always teased her that I wouldn't allow her to stop the filming and instead would prop her up on the motorbike like Charlton Heston in the grand finale of *El Cid*. When she went into hospital we had filmed four out of eight programmes for the fourth series, although we hadn't recorded the crucial voice-over for them. It was Jennifer who was determined that they should be finished and, propped up in bed and encouraged by Rex, her much-loved sound recordist, she gave the performance of a lifetime, waving away visitors and nurses with a haughty "I'm recording for the BBC, you'll have to come back later."

Jennifer's Catholic faith was very powerful and she was convinced that she was heading for a better place. "None of my family have ever been scared of death," she told me. Her conversations were peppered with tales of her beloved saints, whom she would call upon in any situation. In Australia I had a sore throat and she came back from Mass with a pendant of St Blaise, who would heal me of this slight irritation. I didn't share her faith but days after Jennifer died, thinking of her, I flicked through the *Oxford Dictionary of Saints*. Turning to the calendar at the back, I looked up 10 August, the day she died. It was the feast day of St Lawrence — patron saint of cooks.

In the Market

Freddie Foster

I knew her for about twenty years. She used to come to our stall more or less every day. It was brilliant. The first thing she wanted was to know our first names. I didn't know her from Adam obviously, and she used to love it. She used to come along and say, "Frederick, what have you got today?" She inspired me because I also serve restaurants while having a stall in Pimlico Market. I showed her things, and she used to tell me whether she thought it would go retail or not. A perfect example of that was a truffle. I had to get truffles for the restaurateur Nico Ladenis, and I had one left over. It cost about £35.

When I got to the stall I didn't know what to do with this truffle. So I said, "Jennifer, what am I going to do with this?" She said, "My dear, put it on the stall, you'll sell it within half an hour. Trust me, trust me." I used to sell wild mushrooms anyway, so I did this beautiful display with the truffle on the top, and she was right, within twenty-five minutes it was sold. I introduced truffles into Pimlico Market for the first time, all because of Jennifer.

What she looked for were things you couldn't buy in supermarkets or normal markets. She loved smoked garlic. I had to tell her who used it, and of course then she would write about it, and then she'd thrust the paper in front of me and say, "Look, I've written about you again."

Another classic example was pots of basil. Out in the wind they wilt. One day she came along and there were about twenty pots on the floor, they were completely dead. She said, "What are you doing with those, Frederick?" I said, "I'm throwing them out, Jennifer, why?" She said, "Don't you dare, give them to me." I said, "Jennifer, they're dead, I said I'm throwing them out." "Give them to me." I forgot all about it.

Two, three weeks go past, she comes along on her moped, of course, with her helmet on, and she's carrying this thing of basil pots, and they were fantastic. I was sure she'd got them from a different place, but she hadn't, she actually saved them and got them going again. And that was what she was about, she wasn't about making things for any sort of profit or gain. She used to come down every single day to the market, and that was her life. Whatever she did later on in the day, the market was the most important thing for her. She'd come to me, and she used to go to Ted Wright, the fishmonger. "Teddy, what fish have you got for me today?" It really livened up what was already a lively market anyway, and of course the people that enjoyed it most were the customers queuing against your stall, because it was like a double act. She would come along, she would say something, I'd say something back, and they'd all be standing there agape.

I never ever saw her without her helmet. She used to come along on the moped, drive straight into the market. No one else was allowed to do that, except Jennifer. Park up outside the stall, and of course you would expect the helmet to come off. But she used to do all her shopping with her helmet on. The only time I actually saw her before she did the television series without her helmet on, I invited her to my daughter's christening in Ebury Street. When she come through the door I couldn't believe it. Is that you? I was expecting the helmet on as well. But that's how she lived, she was so natural. People might think it was a put-on, but it wasn't. And that was her charm. She was all sincerity.

She used to tell us all the time how she'd been sacked from this paper and that paper, and then one day she came up and said, "You will not believe what the BBC want me to do now." "What's that, Jennifer?" She said, "They want me to drive in this monstrosity of a motorbike with another fat woman as pillion. It will never take off." I said, "Is that just going to be a one-off, Jennifer?" She said, "I hope so." And you know the rest of the story. That's her character, you know. Probably when she got that part to do, she just did it because she enjoyed it, she thought it would be fun. She never thought it would be a success, she just thought it would be fun.

I don't think she changed at all when she became famous. The television never showed how wonderful she was in real life, but even so she came across so much more vividly than most people on television. She was a born natural, there's no doubt about it, and I'll miss her.

Enter the Two Fat Ladies

Clarissa Dickson Wright

The portion of my life occupied by Jennifer is an astonishingly brief five years and due entirely to the imagination of one whom Jennifer used to describe as a Welsh wizard, Pat Llewellyn. As Pat is undoubtedly related to Llewellyn ap Llewellyn, the last true Prince of Wales, who also bore that title, it is singularly apt.

Let me set to rest certain myths: Jennifer and I were not old friends and we were certainly not, as the press would have had it, an item. We had met once at a lunch party in Tuscany five years before. The only reason Jennifer came to talk to me was because I was baking pizzas in an old bread oven. "So Boy Scout," she would say — she was endlessly curious.

I had met Pat Llewellyn when she was assistant producer on Sophie Grigson's *Eat your Greens*; she had filmed me with my cardoons and we had become friends and had often talked about making television together. Basil Comley, who had worked with Jennifer, introduced her to Pat to add to her collection of large posh ladies of a certain age and as Jennifer had driven away on her motorbike Pat had had a vision. Very prone to visions the Welsh!

I was summoned to London for lunch at Simply Nico's, a restaurant much loved by Jennifer as she could "go home by rail", as one of my friends used to refer to following the railings home after too good a meal. I had no concept as to how I would get on with Jennifer; pre-Vatican II devoutly Catholic fruit flies are not high on my guest wish list. Following lunch, although I thought the idea was great, I was still unsure. Jennifer playing the Jennifer she had designed as her façade against the world was undoubtedly funny, sometimes cruel and, while wonderful for television, rather overpowering in a confined space. I had doubted the BBC would even look at the idea but Michael Jackson, to my surprise, commissioned a pilot.

The day of the pilot dawned, and we set off for the Holland and Holland shooting school in north London. It must have been daunting for Jennifer as she had never driven a motorbike and sidecar but she was a splendid trooper and never showed it. It was a filthy day and we pottered around with umbrellas and shotguns. The rain cleared off in the afternoon and they wheeled out the bike. Not the Black Prince that carried us to fame on TV but an old AJS with a sidecar distinctly resembling a coffin. Fortunately I missed the trial run where Jennifer ended up in a ditch and we had three perfect runs at it.

Pat as ever demanded one more shot and this time the bike took off like a bat out of hell with Jennifer's cut-glass vowels conveying all too clearly the words "Oh my God, I can't stop it, it's gone mad!" So comforting. We were heading straight for a brick wall, in front of which stood Pat and the camera crew, at what seemed like 100mph. At the last minute Jennifer swung the bike away, side-swiped the camera, and we were off again heading for three flag poles which we wedged between with a sickening thud and no more than superficial damage. They rolled us back to do our piece to camera. Pat, quite unshaken and relentless, pressed on; Jennifer, quite used to little accidents on bikes, was undaunted; and only I, without the benefit of nicotine or brandy, was left shaken.

The second day of the pilot was the one where we were to cook together, and owing to a flooded burglar alarm we sat and waited together for two hours. It was the first time I had been alone with Jennifer and it was there I discovered the person who was to be my professional friend for the next four years. The real Jennifer without the façade of braggadocio and panache, without the glass barrier of alcohol, was rather a cosy person. She loved a good gossip. Her friends and her religion were the cornerstones of her existence and, once I had told her my story, she was enormously defensive of my recovery and would spring to my protection whenever she perceived a threat.

I could not have worked happily for those years with the public Jennifer, but here I found my good companion. I think they thought we would fight on screen — two opinionated women of a certain age. However, I don't know in what previous life we were best friends but what you saw was what you got. Pat Llewellyn rode us on a very light rein: she pointed us and let us run where we would, but one knew one was never off the bit.

So the programme was commissioned and off we set on our adventures. The first programme, at Mevagissey, nearly did for us all. Pat had assumed at that point that we would be scripted and turned up with a scenario which included the word "toothsome". This reduced Jennifer and me to tears of near collapse and for the first time of many we hysterically clung to one another giggling like school girls and repeating, "Toothsome — no, dear, I insist you say it" as Pat stood looking rather miffed. We spent the rest of the series trying to introduce the word at unsuitable moments. The first shooting morning we mobbed up the script, so much that Pat, quivering with anger, said, "If you're so clever, do it yourselves", and we did, under her guiding hand, for the next three and a half years.

Mevagissey was a nightmare. The first day was lost in mist, which meant that to catch up we were filming the cooking sequences at 2a.m.; again without stimulants, I waned. Jennifer was great: "What you need, dear, is a song" and she would bellow and break into Noël Coward or Duggie Byng. She was particularly pleased if I got a song stuck in my head — her two great achievements were "the Baby in the West Wing" from a verse in "The Stately Homes of England" and, still worse, "All Day Through I Think of You", which I carried for a whole year with top-ups from Jennifer.

Programme two, filmed at Westonbirt girls' school, saw the famous 180-degree turn. Jennifer had been a biker for thirty-five years and when she wasn't playing the frail heroine to Steve the bike boy, on whom she had the most monumental crush, she was very good at it. She was always encouraging him to teach her new tricks. On this occasion I wasn't aware what she was going to do and neither was Pat, who rushed over afterwards to protest that we weren't insured for stunts; so reassuring.

The series went out and we became an overnight success. Pat had translated all our quirks and passions to screen flawlessly and added her own wit and talent in that presentation. *Two Fat Ladies* is a gem of television: it won endless technical awards. I suspect the reason it never won any of the food awards was the jealousy with which the food world is rife. Pat minded; Jennifer and I didn't really care.

Ours was the only cookery series to translate worldwide. We were huge in the USA — fourth best-selling book in Los Angeles (they must have read it for pornography); seventy per cent of the Australian viewing audience watched us; we were dubbed into Japanese using men's voices (Japanese women have little breathy voices); subtitled into Hebrew; it went on and on.

I suspect it was the tours — Australia for ten days and the USA twice — that did for Jennifer. They nearly killed me too with exhaustion. Australia was amazing: rooms full of eight hundred people screaming. Jennifer said she felt like a cross between the Queen Mother and the Beatles. In Australia we felt loved. America was different: we just felt exploited — only one book signing to meet our fans and that was cut short for a journalistic interview. We made a rap video, though, which was fun — I think they were amazed at how fluidly we danced.

The three of us Pat, Jennifer and I, were inseparable through all the weird and wonderful experiences. Jennifer was ever one for the line that took your breath away. I remember driving through London in some parade in a vintage Bentley with cheering crowds and Jennifer remarking, "Now I know how Hitler felt." You never knew what she would say next and that, I suppose, was the fun of it all.

Jennifer once told me that when she was a little girl she wanted to be the lady in the circus who wore a pink tutu and rode round on the Rossenback with all the spotlights on her — which is why the day after her death Pat and I were to be seen weeping in Charlotte Street with me exclaiming, "But you gave her the Rossenback." She loved every minute of the fame and the spotlights — the lorry drivers giving her the thumbs up as she rode Ruby, her motorbike. I shall never really forgive her family for vetoing the horse-drawn hearse with black plumes. Jennifer was high camp till the last.

The Spouting Well of Joy

A. N. Wilson

As well as the grief and the shock — when we heard the dreadful news that Jennifer had a very short time left — there was something else in store. Something which turned out to be wonderful. The hundreds who trooped to that spontaneous bedside party in hospital encountered a woman who was staring death in the face. She did so without flinching. Without self-importance or self-dramatization. I will never forget this, and I'm sure this is true for everyone who saw her in those last weeks and days.

There was nothing phoney about Jennifer. "The spouting well of joy within that never yet was dried" sprang from something very deep.

She had a huge capacity for friendship — witness the size of this crowd. The names of her friends peppered her conversation — without explanation, usually. It was baffling if you didn't know whom she was talking about. We had not always met one another. My beloved Patricius, darling Milo, beloved Paul, my beloved Clare, darling Francis — and so on — the names were just there like catalogues of martyrs in the canon of the Mass.

She loved her married friends to have babies and children just as much as she hated them to have dogs. She was good with children. She remembered small details. She remembered birthdays. My wife's birthday always began with the telephone ringing and Jennifer singing, "Happy birthday to you!" Hundreds of others had the same experience. Most loved it. In the case of some — such as the famous politicians to whom she did it — one suspected a strong element of tease.

It's the octave of the Assumption and I've been thinking how Jennifer, like Our Lady, enjoyed the idea of putting down the mighty from their seats. Not in the spirit of political subversion. She was the Highest of Tories. More in the spirit of prank. Perhaps taking their seats away from them before they'd even sat down.

Her rudeness — and it could be breathtaking — was that of a child. It completely lacked malice.

Like a child, she made artlessly personal remarks. Her first remark to me — before we had even been introduced some twenty years ago — "Darlin' — do you realize you've got a spot on the end of your nose?"

Like a child.

She had an enormous capacity for love — not merely for showing love, with her great bear hugs and her loud "Hallo, darlin'" — but for inspiring it too. There have been many tears shed by her friends over her death. Once, when we were sitting, the three of us, beloved Clare Asquith, she and I, Jennifer prophesied that she would die at about sixty-three or -four. I noticed that a few years later she was discussing plans for a possible seventieth birthday party. But she wasn't flinching from death when she postponed it.

She appeared to live for the present moment. She loved parties, jokes, friends — above all friends. She did not appear to be eaten up by regret or ambition. Laughter and the love of friends were the keystones of her life. But she loved life without illusion. She prepared herself for the hour of her death — long before her last illness. She spoke of it often.

Yet we, the hundreds of friends, took her so for granted.

We knew she was a certain age and that she smoked and drank but we thought that the funny songs and the party would go on for ever. London life is hardly imaginable without her.

I haven't mentioned the world of work: the *Spectator* lunches which she cooked during the golden years of Alexander Chancellor's editorship and Algy Cluff's proprietorship. Who will forget her egg mousse, her fish pie, her sublime oxtail stew, jugged hare — the best — or those scrummy convent eggs?

She was sacked many times, but her policy on such occasions was just to turn up for work as normal the next morning. If her noise or her naughtiness became intolerable, Alexander, kindest of men, used to say that the day he'd chosen to sack her would invariably turn out to be something like his birthday. He'd turn up to the office sternly certain that this would be the day when he told her that this time she was sacked for good. But she'd be standing there on the stairs with a present hidden behind her smock and the inevitable "Happy birthday to you, happy birthday to you!"

I don't need to say anything about the telly. It was lovely for her to have some fame and some money at the end — but her life had not been a pursuit of either. She had — and she gave — tremendous fun. *Two Fat Ladies* was really just an extension of her playful social life. Laughter and the love of friends were the important things. Now and at the hour of our death.

How proud we should all be if at that inevitable hour we could look back on a life led with comparable joy, or forward to a death faced with comparable courage.

The first time I went to see her in hospital, I dreaded it. And of course I asked the tomfool question, "How are you?" "Oh — dying," she said. After we'd chatted a bit she said she was going to the bathroom. I said I'd leave. But no, she said, stay. The door closed, and I heard her burst, quite spontaneously and cheerfully, into one of her favourite Cole Porter numbers: "Another Opening to Another Show".

ISIS publish a wide range of books in large print, from fiction to biography. A full list of titles is available free of charge from the address below. Alternatively, contact your local library for details of their collection of ISIS large print books.

Details of ISIS complete and unabridged audio books are also available.

Any suggestions for books you would like to see in large print or audio are always welcome.

7 Centremead
Osney Mead
Oxford OX2 0ES
(01865) 250333